Domestic Terrorism

by Carla Mooney

LUCENT BOOKS
A part of Gale, Cengage Learning

GALE
CENGAGE Learning·

Farmington Hills, Mich • San Francisco • New York • Waterville, Maine
Meriden, Conn • Mason, Ohio • Chicago

LIBRARY OF CONGRESS CATALOGING-IN-PUBLICATION DATA

Mooney, Carla, 1970-
  Domestic terrorism / by Carla Mooney.
     pages cm. -- (Hot topics)
  Includes bibliographical references and index.
  ISBN 978-1-4205-1219-9 (hardcover)
  1. Domestic terrorism--United States. 2. Domestic terrorism. I. Title.
  HV6432.M649 2014
  363.3250973--dc23
                                          2014019370

Lucent Books
27500 Drake Rd.
Farmington Hills, MI 48331
ISBN-13: 978-1-4205-1219-9
ISBN-10: 1-4205-1219-6

Printed in the United States of America
1 2 3 4 5 6 7 18 17 16 15 14

CONTENTS

FOREWORD   4

INTRODUCTION   6

CHAPTER 1   11
What Is Domestic Terrorism?

CHAPTER 2   27
Islamic Terrorists in the United States

CHAPTER 3   40
Eco-Terrorism

CHAPTER 4   54
Domestic Terror Online

CHAPTER 5   68
Preventing Domestic Terrorism

CHAPTER 6   81
The Future of Domestic Terrorism

NOTES   94

DISCUSSION QUESTIONS   102

ORGANIZATIONS TO CONTACT   104

FOR MORE INFORMATION   106

INDEX   108

PICTURE CREDITS   111

ABOUT THE AUTHOR   112

FOREWORD

Young people today are bombarded with information. Aside from traditional sources such as newspapers, television, and the radio, they are inundated with a nearly continuous stream of data from electronic media. They send and receive e-mails and instant messages, read and write online blogs, participate in chat rooms and forums, and surf the web for hours. This trend is likely to continue. As Patricia Senn Breivik, the former dean of university libraries at Wayne State University in Detroit, has stated, "Information overload will only increase in the future. By 2020, for example, the available body of information is expected to double every 73 days! How will these students find the information they need in this coming tidal wave of information?"

Ironically, this overabundance of information can actually impede efforts to understand complex issues. Whether the topic is abortion, the death penalty, gay rights, or obesity, the deluge of fact and opinion that floods the print and electronic media is overwhelming. The news media report the results of polls and studies that contradict one another. Cable news shows, talk radio programs, and newspaper editorials promote narrow viewpoints and omit facts that challenge their own political biases. The World Wide Web is an electronic minefield where legitimate scholars compete with the postings of ordinary citizens who may or may not be well informed or capable of reasoned argument. At times, strongly worded testimonials and opinion pieces both in print and electronic media are presented as factual accounts.

Conflicting quotes and statistics can confuse even the most diligent researchers. A good example of this is the question of whether or not the death penalty deters crime. For instance, one study found that murders decreased by nearly one-third when the death penalty was reinstated in New York in 1995. Death penalty supporters cite this finding to support their argument that the existence of the death penalty deters criminals from committing murder. However, another study found that states without the death penalty have murder rates below the national average. This study is cited by opponents of capital punishment, who reject the claim that the death penalty deters murder. Students need context and clear, informed discussion if they are to think critically and make informed decisions.

The Hot Topics series is designed to help young people wade through the glut of fact, opinion, and rhetoric so that they can think critically about controversial issues. Only by reading and thinking critically will they be able to formulate a viewpoint that is not simply the parroted views of others. Each volume of the series focuses on one of today's most pressing social issues and provides a balanced overview of the topic. Carefully crafted narrative, fully documented primary and secondary source quotes, informative sidebars, and study questions all provide excellent starting points for research and discussion. Full-color photographs and charts enhance all volumes in the series. With its many useful features, the Hot Topics series is a valuable resource for young people struggling to understand the pressing issues of the modern era.

INTRODUCTION

On April 15, 2013, 23,000 runners lined up for the 117th running of the Boston Marathon. The sun shone brightly as the runners made their way along the 26.2-mile (42.2km) course from Hopkinton, Massachusetts, to Boston's Back Bay neighborhood. Thousands of spectators lined the course, holding signs of encouragement and cheering on family, friends, and strangers.

Amid the festivities, few people noticed two young men as they walked down Boston's Boylston Street toward the finish line shortly after 2:30 PM The two men, one wearing a black baseball hat and the other wearing a backwards white hat, carried large backpacks. As the men walked, they stopped casually, placed the bags on the ground, and walked away.

At 2:49 PM, more than 17,000 runners had already crossed the finish line and approximately 5,700 runners were still on the course. Spectators crowded to watch the runners finish. Suddenly, the afternoon's peace was shattered as an explosion ripped through the sidelines. Twelve seconds later, a second explosion detonated a little over 200 yards (183m) from the first. Laughter turned to screams as the crowd panicked. The wounded lay crumpled on the ground and blood stained the area. As sirens erupted, rescuers leapt into action.

First responders help the victims of two explosions near the finish line of the Boston Marathon, on Monday, April 15, 2013, in Massachusetts. Five people were killed and 267 were injured in the attack.

Minutes after the explosions, Boston Police Commissioner Ed Davis received a call from his superintendent-in-chief, Daniel Linskey. "I'm not sure what we got, boss," Linskey said, "but I think it's bad." Davis says he knew at that moment they were dealing with terrorism. "I started to operate on the premise it was an attack,"[1] he says. Thousands of police officers and law enforcement from dozens of agencies jumped into action, securing the crime scene and investigating the attack. Five people died in the Marathon bombing, and 267 more were injured.

That day, the entire city of Boston was shut down. A no-fly zone was enforced over the bombing sites, major sporting events were canceled, and SWAT team members with machine guns patrolled hospitals where the injured were treated. Three hours after the explosions, President Barack Obama spoke to the nation. "We will find out who did this. We'll find out why they did this," he said. "Any responsible individuals, any responsible groups, will feel the full weight of justice."[2]

Investigators Gather Clues

Over the next few days, investigators built a picture of the attack. They meticulously documented every piece of evidence found within the fifteen-block zone shut down by police. They bagged and sent the evidence to a crime lab for analysis. By examining the debris found at the bombing site, investigators determined the bombs were made from ordinary kitchen pressure cookers packed with explosives, nails, and ball bearings. The attackers hid the bombs in black backpacks and left them on the sidewalks near the race finish line.

Investigators also pored through thousands of photographs and videos from residents, tourists, and businesses at the scene, searching for those responsible for the attack. They replayed video footage, searching through the crowds for individuals who seemed out of place with those around them. "The sheer volume of stuff made it difficult to sort through," says Colonel Tim Alben of the Massachusetts State Police. Even so, "we were very confident that there were enough cameras down there that we were going to capture something."[3]

By April 18, investigators narrowed their focus to two young men. They did not know who they were, but they revealed photos and video of the men to the public. A few hours later, the two men engaged in a gunfight on the Massachusetts Institute of Technology (MIT) campus, killing an MIT campus police officer. The suspects carjacked a vehicle and led the police on a chase that ended in Watertown, Massachusetts. The suspects threw explosive devices from the car and exchanged gunfire with police. In the mayhem, one suspect was shot and killed. The second suspect escaped but was later tracked down in a massive manhunt and arrested.

Domestic Terrorists

Over the next days and weeks, investigators searched into the backgrounds of the suspects, twenty-six-year-old Tamerlan Tsarnaev and his nineteen-year-old brother Dzhokhar, to learn what had motivated them to carry out the bombing. Many details were ordinary, showing a picture of two young immigrants adjusting to life in the United States. The Tsarnaev brothers arrived in the United States in 2003 from the former Soviet Union. They lived in Cambridge, Massachusetts, and appeared to be embracing American life. Tamerlan was a competitive boxer and an aspiring engineer. The younger brother, Dzhokhar, attended a prestigious public high school and became a U.S. citizen in 2012. He was registered as a student at the University of Massachusetts Dartmouth.

Investigators also uncovered troubling details about the brothers. Although he had been in the United States for several years, Tamerlan was reported to have said that he did not have a single American friend. Investigators discovered that in 2012 Tamerlan had traveled to Dagestan, a volatile region in southern Russia that is known for a violent struggle with Islamist insurgency. Investigators believed that Tamerlan had traveled to the region to make contact with militant groups, but for an unknown reason did not join any groups.

Investigators believe the brothers were motivated by extremist Islamic beliefs even though they were not acting on the behalf of any known foreign terrorist groups. Instead, the brothers were homegrown. While living in the United States, they became violent extremists and used the Internet to learn how to build bombs. "The increasing signals are that these were individuals who were radicalized, especially the older brother, over a period of time—radicalized by Islamist fundamentalist terrorists, basically using Internet sources to gain not just the types of philosophical beliefs that radicalized them, but also learning components of how to do these sorts of things," says Senator Marco Rubio of Florida, who serves on the Senate Intelligence Committee. "This is a new element of terrorism that we have to face in our country," Mr. Rubio says. "We need to be prepared for Boston-type attacks, not just 9/11-type attacks."[4]

Targeting Civilians

Almost every day, television news shows, newspapers, and radio broadcasts run stories and display images of violent attacks like the Boston Marathon bombing. While most people think of the September 11, 2001, attacks on New York, Washington, D.C., and rural Pennsylvania when talking about terrorism, domestic terrorism has been an issue in the United States for generations. "Actually, the majority of terrorist acts have no connections to the Middle East or Asia, but are strictly home-grown, originating with American citizens who are left- or right-wing extremists, animal activists, environmental radicals, anti-abortion extremists. Most are committed by American citizens,"[5] says Jack Levin, a professor of sociology and criminology at Northeastern University.

Extremists of all types, acting alone or in groups, have turned to terrorism as a way to achieve specific goals or to get their message to the public. "The Boston bombings are a reminder that there are evil, violent people out there who are willing to murder an 8-year-old boy, maim innocent bystanders, and deliberately target ordinary citizens," said Andrew Liepman, a former principal deputy director of the National Counterterrorism Center and a senior policy analyst at the RAND Corporation, a nonprofit global think tank:

> I expect we'll know more soon about their motives—but on some level, I'm not even sure I care that much. What's the difference if they ascribe this atrocity to a neo-Nazi, radical Islamist, or separatist anti-government ideology? Whatever their motive, they're cowardly murderers who need to be brought to justice.[6]

WHAT IS DOMESTIC TERRORISM?

M illions of people who support various causes, issues, and political agendas use legal methods to send a message to governments and citizens. Activists organize protests and rallies and circulate petitions for a wide variety of causes ranging from animal rights to abortion. They participate in the political process, voting for candidates and advocating laws that agree with their beliefs.

In extreme cases, some people have turned to violence in the name of their beliefs. These individuals and groups plan and carry out violent attacks against civilians, government officials, and other targets, using bombs, guns, or other weapons to demand change.

Violence Against Civilians

Domestic terrorism is defined as any terrorist activity that occurs within a homeland. According to the Federal Bureau of Investigation (FBI), domestic terrorism has three characteristics. First, it involves acts that are dangerous to human life and violate state or federal law. Second, it primarily occurs within a country or its areas of territorial jurisdiction. Finally, domestic terrorism is designed to intimidate or coerce civilians, influence government policy, or affect government conduct. Many terrorist acts are related to a larger political objective. The anti-abortion activist who seeks the end of legalized abortions and the homegrown jihadist, someone who supports a holy war to spread Muslim beliefs and wants to end U.S. military operations overseas, are both examples of domestic terrorists.

TERRORIST INCIDENTS IN THE UNITED STATES

Number of terrorist incidents in the United States from 1995 to 2011 by perpetrator ideology

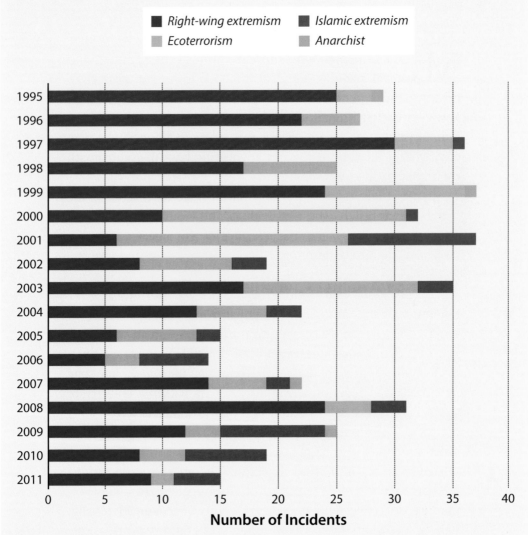

Source: Ken Sofer and Molly Bernstein, "Chart: 17 Years After Oklahoma City Bombing, Right-Wing Extremism Is Significant Domestic Terror Threat," ThinkProgress, April 19, 2012. http://thinkprogress.org/security /2012/04/19/467384/chart-right-wing-extremism-terror-threat-oklahoma-city.

Although domestic terrorism involves illegal acts, it has several key differences from other criminal activity. Regular criminals generally operate in the shadows. They go to great lengths to hide their involvement in a crime. For example, a murderer will hide a body or remove incriminating evidence from a crime scene. A thief might wear a disguise to conceal his or her identity. In addition, regular criminals often are motivated by personal or financial reasons. In many cases, the criminal has a personal connection to victims.

In contrast, domestic terrorists plan their attacks so that they will be widely publicized. Attacks often are designed to create the maximum amount of fear and chaos, with the goal of capturing the attention of a city, state, or country. Bombings, kidnappings, and mass shootings are all tactics that domestic terrorists use to gain attention for their cause. In addition, domestic terrorists rarely have personal connections to their victims. Instead, victims of domestic terror attacks usually are chosen randomly. These men, women, and children have the bad luck of being in the wrong place at the wrong time. The 1995 Oklahoma City bombing was a grim reminder that anyone could become a victim of domestic terror. The bombing was a domestic terror attack on the Alfred P. Murrah Federal Building in Oklahoma City on April 19. Timothy McVeigh, an American militia sympathizer who hated the federal government, detonated the bomb in a rental truck parked in front of the building with the help of co-conspirator Terry Nichols. In the bombing of the federal building, 168 people were killed, including nineteen children who attended a daycare center in the building.

Domestic terrorism comes in many forms. Individuals and groups from various religious, ethnic, and political background, from the Ku Klux Klan in the southern United States to eco-terrorists in Oregon, have been involved in terrorist attacks in the United States. Often, these people and groups have not been able to reach their goals of political or social change through traditional, nonviolent means. As a result, they view violence and terrorism as the way to achieve them.

The Unabomber

Over the course of almost two decades, Theodore Kaczynski, known as the Unabomber, delivered sixteen mail bombs that killed three people and injured twenty-three others. A brilliant mathematician, Kaczynski suffered social and emotional problems and lived as a hermit in Montana. He developed a radical environmental philosophy and an opposition to modern technology. The rejection of one of his academic essays by two Chicago universities in 1978 may have triggered Kaczynski's violence.

In 1978, a security guard at Northwestern University was seriously injured when he opened a suspicious package. Over the next eighteen years, there were fifteen more bombs, targeting universities and airlines. Some explosions killed people nearby. In 1995, Kaczynski sent a manifesto to major newspapers saying he would stop killing if they published it. The *Washington Post* published the "Unabomber's Manifesto," which detailed what Kaczynski thought to be problems in U.S. society. When Kaczynski's brother read the manifesto, he recognized his brother's ideas and language. The brother notified the FBI he suspected Ted was the Unabomber. In April 1996, the FBI arrested Ted Kaczynski at his Montana cabin. Kaczynski pled guilty to more than a dozen federal charges. He was sentenced to four life sentences plus thirty years in prison.

Homegrown Jihadists

Since the September 11 attacks, Americans have been on alert to the threat from violent Islamic extremists. Islamic extremists believe in promoting a radical version of Islamic law and using violence against non-Muslim civilians. Often, Islamic extremists believe Western countries, led by the United States, are at war with Islam. As a result, some believers seek to kill large numbers of Americans by any means possible. Many Islamic extremists are willing to die for their cause, which makes them one of the most dangerous terroristic threats in the United States.

Prior to the September 11 attacks on New York City and Washington, D.C., and that led to the plane crash in rural Pennsylvania, foreign-born, Islamic extremists gathered in terror camps in the Middle East to train, organize, and plan attacks on

Western sites. More than a decade later, Islamic extremists have become more decentralized. In some cases, citizens of Western nations travel to Middle Eastern camps for training. Then they return to their home countries to carry out terrorist attacks. Other times, Western-born Islamic extremists use the Internet to plan attacks from their homes. These homegrown Islamic extremists are encouraged to strike in the United States when the opportunity arises. According to Brian Michael Jenkins, senior advisor to the president of the RAND Corporation, in a briefing to newly elected members of Congress in 2011:

> Al Qaeda now places increased emphasis on do-it-yourself terrorism, urging local would-be jihadists to do whatever they can wherever they are. Without experience or practical instruction, homegrown terrorists have not achieved the sophistication of centrally supported efforts, but they have learned that attacks at home, even when unsuccessful, still cause great alarm.[7]

Despite the headlines Islamic extremism receives, there have been relatively few terrorist attacks by these groups in the United States in recent years. According to Gordon Lederman, chief counsel for national security and investigations of the U.S. Senate Homeland Security and Governmental Affairs Committee, there were only fifty-three cases of homegrown violent Islamist extremism between September 11, 2011, and June 2012:

> To be sure, these cases of homegrown violent Islamist extremism represent a tiny percentage of the estimated 6 million Muslim-Americans. Moreover, as Presidents George W. Bush and Barack Obama have stressed since 9/11, the United States is not at war with Islam but rather with adherents to an ideology that perverts it.[8]

Militia Extremists

Another group that has conducted terrorist attacks in the United States is militia extremists. Organized into paramilitary groups with a military-like hierarchy, militia extremists believe that they are protecting the U.S. Constitution, other laws, and their personal liberty. They oppose government policies and believe U.S. citizens have the right to take back the government by force if it becomes necessary. They tend to stockpile illegal weapons and ammunition, including fully automatic firearms, and buy or make improvised explosive devices (IEDs). Because they value weaponry, militia extremists often oppose gun control efforts and see gun control as an attempt by the government to disarm citizens.

THE THREAT WITHIN

"My greatest fear is that domestic extremists in this country will somehow become emboldened to the point of carrying out a mass-casualty attack, because they perceive that no one is being vigilant about the threat from within. That is what keeps me up at night."—Daryl Johnson, former senior domestic terrorism analyst for the Department of Homeland Security

Quoted in Heidi Beirich. "Inside the DHS: Former Top Analyst Says Agency Bowed to Political Pressure." Southern Poverty Law Center, Summer 2011. www.splcenter.org /get-informed/intelligence-report/browse-all-issues/2011/summer/inside-the-dhs -former-top-analyst-says-agency-bowed.

Militia extremists often target government officials, law enforcement, court personnel, and government buildings. In March 2010, nine members of a militia extremist group were arrested in Michigan and charged with seditious conspiracy, attempted use of weapons of mass destruction, teaching the use of explosive materials, and possessing a firearm during a crime of violence. According to their indictment, the individuals planned to kill a law enforcement officer and then attack a caravan of cars in the officer's funeral procession with bombs in an attempt to cause an armed conflict with law enforcement. The FBI and Michigan state police were able to stop and arrest the suspects before they could carry out the plan. "This is an example of radical and extremist fringe groups which can be found throughout our society. The FBI takes such extremist groups seriously, especially those who would target innocent citizens and the law enforcement officers who protect the citizens of the United States,"[9] says FBI special agent in charge Andrew Arena.

Anarchists

Anarchy is a belief that society would be better off with no government, laws, police, or authority of any kind. Some anarchists oppose business, globalism, and urbanization. While many anarchists work for change through nonviolent, legal tactics, a smaller number of anarchists believe terroristic tactics are needed to effect change.

Unlike militia extremists, who are organized in paramilitary groups with a defined hierarchy, anarchist extremists usually have no central leadership and are loosely organized. Typically, these individuals target symbols of Western civilization they blame for

A group of protesters who had turned violent loots a coffee shop during the 1999 World Trade Organization Summit in Seattle, Washington.

society's problems, such as financial corporations and government entities. They often focus their efforts on large events such as political conventions, economic and financial summits, and environmental meetings. To bring attention to their cause, they may damage and vandalize property, set fires, use small bombs, and start riots.

At the 1999 World Trade Organization meetings in Seattle, Washington, protesters organized a rally to protest global capitalism. While many protesters attended the rally peacefully, a small group of extremists turned violent, disrupting the meetings, looting, and damaging property. Police responded to the violence with pepper spray, tear gas, and a curfew, as they attempted to regain control of Seattle streets. "It was chaos in the streets,"[10] says Jerry Jasinowski, president of the National Association of Manufacturers, who attended the conference.

Sovereign Citizens

Sovereign citizens hold antigovernment beliefs. They believe they are separate or sovereign from the United States, even though they physically live within the country's borders. As sovereign citizens, these individuals believe most branches of the federal government are illegitimate entities with no authority over them. Many of these individuals do not pay taxes, have a driver's license, or carry a Social Security card. Additionally, they do not recognize the authority of the police or the court system.

A sovereign citizen for almost thirty years, Alfred Adask says the sovereign citizen movement has grown in recent years. "What's driving people to it is they're beginning to understand that the government has moved away from fundamental principles that this nation was built on. Where are the limits in limited government? The sovereignty movement is attempting to rediscover those limits and reassert them,"[11] says Adask.

Many sovereign citizens fight the system with paperwork. These people file liens or financial claims against the personal assets of police officers or judges to ruin their credit. Others have been accused of crimes such as impersonating police of-

Olympic Park Bombing

On July 27, 1996, a bomb exploded in Centennial Olympic Park, disrupting the XXVI Summer Olympics in Atlanta, Georgia. The explosion killed one person and injured more than one hundred others. Even though an anonymous caller had tipped off police to the nail-laden bomb prior to the explosion, police were unable to stop it because it exploded before the caller said it would. Police believed the bomber intended to target law enforcement.

A few months later in January 1997, another nail-laden bomb exploded outside an abortion clinic in an Atlanta suburb. After police and emergency responders arrived at the scene, a second blast exploded, injuring seven people. The next month, a bomb exploded near a crowded gay and lesbian nightclub in Atlanta, injuring several people. Investigators linked the bombings to a single bomber, but did not identify the suspect.

In January 1998, a Birmingham, Alabama, abortion clinic was bombed, killing a police officer and critically wounding a nurse. A tip led investigators to Eric Robert Rudolph, a thirty-one-year-old carpenter. Investigators linked Rudolph to the Birmingham and Atlanta bombings and launched a manhunt. For five years, Rudolph escaped capture by hiding in the North Carolina mountains. In May 2003, he was finally captured. He pled guilty to four bombings and the 1998 murder of a police officer and was sentenced to life in prison.

Flowers and other items decorate the site of the Olympic Park bombing during the 1996 Summer Games in Atlanta, Georgia.

ficers, using counterfeit money, and forging passports, license plates, and driver's licenses. A few sovereign citizens have resorted to violence in the name of their beliefs. Extremists have been involved in violent crimes including murder, assault, and threatening judges, law enforcement, and other government personnel. According to the FBI, sovereign citizens have become one of the country's top domestic terror threats.

Some sovereign citizens believe that violence is unavoidable when dealing to the U.S. government. Adask says that while he does not advocate violence, he believes that the threat of violence makes people listen to his message. "I'm simply saying, one of the ways you prevent the misconstruction or abuse of the powers of the constitution is by letting the people in Washington understand that you are armed. That's the idea behind this. It's saying, 'Look, we're armed down here, don't mess with us,'" he says. "You know, I find it troubling that the government would try to restrict our right to keep and bear arms. The threat of violence is required because they will not listen. The system will not listen to people like me unless there are other people that back me up who have guns,"[12] he adds.

Environmental and Animal Rights Extremists

Since the 1970s, an increasing amount of domestic terrorism activity has been carried out by groups and individuals who support animal rights and environmental protection. Radical groups have carried out attacks on a variety of targets, including international corporations, lumber companies, animal testing facilities, and genetic research firms. Since 1979, environmental and animal rights extremists have committed more than two thousand crimes, causing economic losses of more than $110 million and making them one of the top domestic terror threats in the United States.

In 2003, members of the Earth Liberation Front (ELF), a militant environmentalist group, set fire to a car dealership in West Covina, California, damaging about forty Hummers and SUVs and causing about $2 million in damages. The attackers vandalized cars and painted ELF slogans on the vehicles. ELF representatives said the dealership was targeted because it profited by selling cars that polluted and killed the natural environment. Steve Reisman, founder of the Southern California Hum-

Rows of burned-out vehicles fill a California Hummer dealership's parking lot in August 2003. The Earth Liberation Front claimed responsibility for the arson attack.

mer Owners' Group, said ELF's tactics had crossed the line from activism to terrorism. "They were trying to scare people into not buying them, but it was criminal, and wrong," he says. "It's one thing to pass out leaflets and to put stickers on cars saying they pollute, but it's another to start setting fire to them."[13]

White Supremacy

Domestic terrorism has also been carried out for decades by white supremacist groups. These groups, such as the the Ku Klux Klan, see the white race as superior to other races. While having this belief is not illegal, threatening others or using violence in support of this belief is illegal. According to the FBI, today's white supremacy extremists belong to a number of different groups. They are motivated by a variety of religious or political beliefs and typically target people of a specific racial, ethnic, or religious background. In April 2014, seventy-three-year-old Frazier Glenn Cross went on a shooting spree outside a Jewish community center and nearby Jewish retirement home near Kansas City, Missouri, that killed three people. Officials say that Cross was a known former senior member of the Ku Klux Klan movement and had made public comments against Jewish people. Other times, white supremacy extremists target the federal government.

ATTACKS ARE RARE

"One thing that ought to be remembered is that attacks like the murder of George Tiller and the shooting at the Holocaust Memorial Museum are rare. We should take care not to rush blindly into creating 'solutions' that are ill-suited to the real problems, that result in poor distributions of scarce resources, or that violate basic freedoms."—Phyllis Gerstenfeld, a professor and chairman of the criminal justice department at California State University, Stanislaus

Phyllis Gerstenfeld. "Don't Overreact." *New York Times*, June 11, 2009. http://roomfor debate.blogs.nytimes.com/2009/06/11/hate-crimes-and-extremist-politics.

White supremacists have been linked to assaults, murders, threats, intimidation, and bombings. Some also also been linked to other crimes to fund their activities such as drug trafficking, bank robbery, and counterfeiting. White supremacy extremists often work alone or in small groups, which makes it harder for law enforcement to find them.

In 2011, four men devised a plan to firebomb the home of an interracial couple in Hardy, Arkansas. The men went to the victims' home and threw three Molotov cocktails at the house. The bombs ignited and damaged the home, but the victims were not injured. The men were arrested and sentenced to varying prison terms. Thomas E. Perez, assistant attorney general for the federal government's Civil Rights Division, commented on the crime after one of the extremists was sentenced to twenty years in prison.

White nationalist Frazier Glenn Miller speaks at an event in North Carolina in 1985. Miller is accused of carrying out the shooting spree in 2014 in which three people were killed at a Jewish community center in Overland, Kansas.

"This defendant not only committed acts of race-based violence, but recruited others to commit these hate-filled crimes as well," said Perez. "There is no place in our society for criminal acts such as these. The Justice Department will continue to vigorously prosecute individuals who commit such atrocious acts."[14]

Anti-Abortion Extremists

Abortion is an issue that many people feel strongly about. Anti-abortion activists want legalized abortion to end and the number of abortions in the United States to decrease. While many in the anti-abortion movement protest the legality of abortion through peaceful methods, some extremists commit crimes in the name of their cause. By attacking abortion providers and clinics, they hope to limit abortion services and reduce the number of abortions in the United States. Between 1997 and 2010, there were sixty-six cases of extreme violence that targeted abortion providers and clinics in the United States, according to the Congressional Research Service. These cases frequently involved tactics that spread fear, such as shootings, bombings, arson, and acid attacks. In some cases, these attacks have turned deadly. Since 1993, eight abortion clinic workers have been murdered by anti-abortion extremists. Many extremists believe that murdering abortion providers is justifiable, because they think it is necessary to protect the lives of unborn children.

In 2012, an abortion clinic in Pensacola, Florida, was fire-bombed and destroyed. Police arrested Bobby Joe Rogers and charged him with arson and damaging a reproductive health facility in connection with the firebombing. The forty-one-year-old Rogers pled guilty to the charges and told investigators that he committed the violent crimes because he had a strong opposition to abortion.

Dangers at Home

Domestic terrorists have killed American citizens and caused millions of dollars of property damage across the United States.

Bystanders react to explosions detonated outside the Atlanta, Georgia, Northside Family Planning Services building in January 1997. Between 1997 and 2010 there were sixty-six cases of extreme violence targeting abortion clinics.

Domestic terror organizations support a wide variety of extremist ideologies and movements. Their targets vary by group and can include civilians, commercial entities, government officials and sites, and military targets. Domestic terrorists have used a variety of weapons and tactics, from bombing and gun attacks to arson and firebombing. Scott Stewart, vice president of analysis at Stratfor, a geopolitical intelligence firm states that:

> While unrelated as far as timing and motive, when taken together [terrorist acts] show that extremist ideologies

subscribed to by certain individuals on the fringes of U.S. society continue to radicalize some to the point that they are willing to take violent action in accordance with those ideologies. Domestic terrorism is thus alive and well.[15]

CHAPTER
2

ISLAMIC TERRORISTS
IN THE UNITED STATES

On November 5, 2009, Major Nidal Malik Hasan walked into the Soldier Readiness Processing Center at the Fort Hood military base in Killeen, Texas. Carrying two guns, Hasan shouted "Allahu Akbar," which means "God is great" in Arabic. Then he sprayed bullets in the center, which was crowded with soldiers returning from or about to be sent overseas. The shooting lasted for about ten minutes before Hasan was shot by police and arrested. His rampage killed thirteen people and wounded more than thirty others, making it the deadliest mass murder at a military base in the United States. "The Intelligence Community considers Major Hasan to be a 'Homegrown Violent Extremist' —a person who may engage in ideologically-motivated terrorist activities in furtherance of political or social objectives promoted by a foreign terrorist organization, but is acting independently of direction of a foreign terrorist organization,"[16] says Secretary of the Army John McHugh. In 2013, a military jury found Hasan guilty of forty-five counts of premeditated murder and attempted premeditated murder. He was later sentenced to death.

Hasan's act of violence shocked the country. Investigators looked into his background, trying to understand how an American army officer had become a domestic terrorist. Born in Virginia and the son of Palestinian immigrants, Hasan graduated from Virginia Tech University and completed training in psychiatry at the Uniformed Services University of the Health Sciences in Bethesda, Maryland, in 2003. In May 2009, he was promoted to the rank of major in the army and transferred to Fort Hood.

The investigation revealed that there were signs that over the years Hasan had become a radical Islamic extremist. In e-mails to known terrorist Anwar al-Awlaki, Hasan stated his support of suicide bombings and killing civilians. "I would assume that [a] suicide bomber whose aim is to kill enemy soldiers or their helpers, but also kills innocents in the process is acceptable,"[17] Hasan wrote in one of the e-mails to Awlaki. Although intelligence agencies intercepted the e-mails between Hasan and Awlaki, they decided not to investigate further. "There was no indication that Major Hasan was planning an imminent attack at all, or that he was directed to do anything,"[18] says one

U.S. President Barack Obama and First Lady Michelle Obama view the Fallen Soldier Memorial at Fort Hood in Killeen, Texas, during a November 2009 ceremony honoring the thirteen people killed in a shooting rampage by Nidal Malik Hasan.

senior investigator. The Fort Hood attacks serve as a chilling reminder of the threat of homegrown Islamic extremists in the United States.

A Country on Alert

Since the September 11 attacks, terrorism analysts and public officials have expressed growing concern over the risk of Muslim citizens and residents of the United States plotting terroristic attacks on American soil, a trend called "homegrown" terrorism. Like Major Hasan or the Tsarnaev brothers accused in the Boston Marathon massacre, homegrown Islamic terrorists have grown up in the United States or have lived in the country for years. They know American customs, speak English, blend in easily, and are often unnoticed by law enforcement.

ISOLATED AND RARE

"The Boston Marathon bombing, like the handful of other terrorist attacks in the U.S. by Muslim-Americans in the dozen years since 9/11, remained an isolated, rare incident—deadly and frightening but not a trigger for an upsurge in violent radicalization."—Charles Kurzman, professor of sociology at the University of North Carolina, Chapel Hill, and a specialist on Islamic movements

Charles Kurzman. "Muslim-American Terrorism in 2013." Triangle Center on Terrorism and Homeland Security, February 5, 2014. http://sites.duke.edu/tcths/files/2013/06/Kurzman_Muslim-American_Terrorism_in_2013.pdf.

While violent Islamic extremists are a small minority of the Muslim population in the country, the threat is real and growing. A number of Muslims, who are both naturalized citizens and American-born, have communicated with extremists linked to al Qaeda and other terrorist groups. Investigators say some of these individuals have attempted to gain terrorist training or carry out attacks inside the United States. The Congressional Research Service (CRS) estimates that there have been sixty-three homegrown violent jihadist plots or attacks in the United States between September 11, 2001, and January 2013.

Experts believe that homegrown Islamic terrorists have become more common partly because of a crackdown by the United States on terrorism overseas. Researchers Ally Pregulman and Emily Burke explain in an April 2012 report on homegrown terrorism for the Center for Strategic and International Studies:

> Before 9/11, al Qaeda was able to operate with reasonable mobility, organize large training camps in Afghanistan and Pakistan, and plan elaborate attacks. However, amplified counterterrorism pressure has greatly limited al Qaeda's mobility and capacity to launch operations and has forced it to increasingly rely on affiliates and individuals to carry out its plans.[19]

In May 2010, thirty-year-old Faisal Shahzad, a naturalized U.S. citizen from Pakistan, drove an SUV into New York City's crowded Times Square and parked the vehicle. The SUV was

New York City police commissioner Raymond W. Kelly speaks to the media about a car bomb in Times Square discovered before it was detonated in May 2010. The surveillance photo behind him helped identify the vehicle.

crammed with dozens of M-88 firecrackers, three propane tanks, a pair of gasoline jugs, and a metal locker filled with fertilizer. The SUV's contents were wired to a pair of alarm clocks, designed to blow up the vehicle and anyone nearby. "It's clear that the intent behind this terrorist act was to kill Americans,"[20] says U.S. Attorney General Eric Holder. The attack was thwarted because a fast-acting street vendor alerted police, who were able to disarm the car bomb before it exploded. Shahzad was arrested at the airport as he tried to flee the country and board a flight to Dubai.

Radicalization

The freedom to practice a chosen religion has been one of the core principles of the United States since its founding. While the large majority of Americans practice their religion peacefully, a small number resort to violence to promote their beliefs. According to terrorism expert Jerome Bjelopera, radicalization is the process of acquiring and holding extremist or jihadist beliefs. Jihadism is an extreme version of Islam, making up less than 1 percent of Islamists. Jihadists believe that they are the only true believers and the rest of the world is full of hostile unbelievers who want to destroy Islam. Jihadists also believe in the establishment of a state run by a Muslim civil and religious leader known as a caliph. A violent jihadist believes that violence must be used against the unbelievers and supports, plots, or engages in violent terrorist activity. While holding jihadist beliefs is not a crime, moving to violent action in support of those beliefs creates a terrorist. "Individuals can become jihadist terrorists by radicalizing and then adopting violence as a tactic,"[21] writes Bjelopera.

Knowing who is likely to become a terrorist is difficult. According to Brian Michael Jenkins:

> There is no easily identifiable terrorist-prone personality, no single path to radicalization and terrorism. Many people may share the same views, but only a handful of the radicals will go further to become terrorists. The transition from radical to terrorist is often a matter of

Prison Radicalization

Experts say the nation's prison system is an environment where certain individuals may radicalize on their way to becoming terrorists. Prison brings together people who may be receptive to antisocial messages. In this captive environment, young men and women can be easily influenced by charismatic, extremist leaders.

Because prisons often have few qualified religious leaders, other inmates with little Islamic training become leaders, sometimes misrepresenting Islam. Prison radicalization extends to other extremist groups as well, including extreme Christian groups, white supremacists, and sovereign citizens.

In 2004, inmate Kevin James, serving time for robbery, led a radical prison group translated as the Assembly of Authentic Islam. He recruited other inmates to join the group. James preached to members that their duty was to target enemies of Islam, including the U.S. government and supporters of Israel. James passed around a document that justified the killing of Islam's enemies. He allegedly worked to establish groups of members outside prison to execute violent attacks.

happenstance. It depends on whom one meets and probably on when that meeting occurs in the arc of one's life.[22]

In the United States, homegrown Islamic extremists frequently come from well-off families and have never committed a crime, which makes it extremely difficult to detect them before an attack occurs. "Historically, the idea that terrorists come from [poor and quasi-literate] backgrounds is a complete myth," says Bruce Hoffman, a counterterrorism expert at Georgetown University. "They are much more likely to be well-educated and come from middle-class and wealthy families."[23] For example, Nidal Malik Hasan, who was charged in the Fort Hood massacre, was a psychiatrist and an army major. "Most Muslims in [the United States] are doing well, so those who have been radicalized tend to come from that class,"[24] says Scott Stewart, vice president for tactical intelligence at Stratfor, a private intelligence analysis organization. Stewart says the affluent background and high community status of these accused terrorists makes it harder for law enforcement to track them.

Factors in Radicalization

According to the Center for Strategic and International Studies, several factors have played a role in radicalizing American Muslims. Since 9/11, the wars in Iraq and Afghanistan have been seen by some in the Muslim community as an attack on Muslims. "This narrative has been persuasive enough to motivate a small but disturbing number of American citizens and legal residents to take up arms to prevent further perceived assaults on Muslims,"[25] write Pregulman and Burke.

In addition, the emergence of the Internet and social media has increased the reach of foreign terror groups, allowing them to recruit and train individuals around the world. For example, some terrorism experts believe online teachings and e-mail communications between Hasan and Anwar al-Awlaki, a known terrorist and radical cleric, helped Hasan move from just holding extreme beliefs to taking violent action.

Individuals who decide to commit an act of domestic terrorism often have the help and encouragement of intermediaries. These intermediaries persuade citizens to radicalize and sometimes to become violent jihadists. They can interact with individuals in person or online and, in some cases, may even be a government informant or undercover agent. Before his death in a U.S. airstrike in 2011, Samir Khan was an editor for *Inspire* magazine. *Inspire* was published to attract would-be jihadists and featured political and how-to articles in an American style. Born in Saudi Arabia, Khan lived in New York and Charlotte, North Carolina. He became radicalized after the September 11 attacks. Khan's publications were reported to have influenced several homegrown Islamic extremists. In one case, army private Naser Abdo was arrested in Texas in 2011 for allegedly plotting a mass shooting and bombing. Law enforcement reported that Abdo had a copy of a bomb-making article from *Inspire*.

Bryant Neal Vinas, born in December 1983 to South American immigrants, is a Muslim convert who says he became radicalized after listening to the recorded lectures of radical cleric Anwar al-Awlaki. In 2007, Vinas flew to Lahore, Pakistan, and traveled to an al Qaeda camp in the country. There he participated in basic weapons and explosives training. He shot machine guns, pistols, and rocket-propelled grenades and learned how to detonate the explosives TNT and C4. Vinas says that with al Qaeda leaders he discussed possible attacks on the Long Island Rail

Abdulhakim Muhammad is escorted to the Pulaski County courthouse in Little Rock, Arkansas. The former Carlos Bledsoe had traveled to Yemen, where he trained with terrorist groups.

Road and a large retail chain. Before he could carry out an attack on American soil, however, the Pakistani police arrested Vinas and turned him over to the FBI. He pled guilty to three terrorism charges: conspiracy to murder U.S. nationals, providing material support to a terrorist group, and receiving training from a terrorist group. Sentenced to life in prison, Vinas has been a witness for the U.S. government and several other governments in other suspected terrorists' cases.

MANY FACES OF TERROR

"We need to remember that terrorism is a tactic practiced by actors from a wide array of ethnic and religious backgrounds who follow various ideologies stretching from anarchism to neo-Nazism. Terrorism does not equal jihadism."—Scott Stewart

Scott Stewart. "Domestic Terrorism: A Persistent Threat in the United States."
, August 23, 2012. www.stratfor.com/weekly/domestic-terrorism-persistent
-threat-united-states.

Some people believe Americans and the Muslim community are not doing enough to prevent radicalization of American Muslims. Melvin Bledsoe, a Memphis businessman, testified at a 2011 Congressional hearing on domestic terrorism. He told lawmakers how his son Carlos, raised Baptist, converted to Islam in college. Carlos Bledsoe traveled to Yemen, where he was trained by terrorist groups to kill. After his return to the United States, Bledsoe carried out a gun attack at a military recruiting center in Little Rock, Arkansas, killing one soldier and wounding another. "Our children are in danger," Mr. Bledsoe warned in his testimony. "It seems to me that Americans are sitting around doing nothing about radical extremists. This is a big elephant in the room."[26]

Exaggerated Threat

Despite the attention paid to homegrown Islamic terrorists, other experts say that the threat to Americans from these groups

Controversial Informants

To fight homegrown terrorism, the FBI uses sting operations, often targeting the Muslim community. The FBI sends informants into the community to spend time in mosques and community centers. There they talk about radical Islam ideas and identify people who accept radical beliefs. Once a suspect is identified, the FBI may run a sting. Sometimes the sting lures the suspect into a fake terror plot, leading to his or her arrest.

Of concern, however, are the people who are being used as informants by the FBI. Some informants have criminal records that include attempted murder, drug dealing, or fraud. In addition, many informants are paid six-figure sums, which may create an incentive for them to entrap a target. Other informants are promised debt forgiveness or the erasure of immigration violations.

In California, FBI informant Craig Monteilh posed as a Muslim and spent time at mosques looking for potential suspects. He is a convicted felon on serious drug charges. Monteilh's apparent terrorist talk alarmed his Muslim targets so much they obtained a restraining order against him and alerted the FBI, not knowing that he was in fact an undercover informant.

has been exaggerated. The large majority of Muslim-Americans do not support violence. "There are more than 3 million Muslims in the United States, and few more than 100 have joined jihad—about one out of every 30,000—suggesting an American Muslim population that remains hostile to jihadist ideology and its exhortations to violence,"[27] says Jenkins.

A 2010 study by researchers at Duke University and the University of North Carolina at Chapel Hill found that a small percentage of Muslim-Americans have undergone radicalization since 9/11. In the eight years since the 9/11 attacks, the study found 139 Muslim-Americans were engaged in or prosecuted for terrorism-related offenses, at a rate of about 17 individuals per year. The researchers concluded that homegrown terrorism was a serious but limited problem. "Muslim-American organizations and the vast majority of individuals that we interviewed firmly reject the radical extremist ideology that justifies the use of violence to achieve political ends,"[28] says David Schanzer, an associate professor in Duke's Sanford School of Public Policy and director of the Triangle Center on Terrorism and Homeland Security.

The threat of domestic terrorism from homegrown Islamic militants is even lower because many attempts are unsuccessful, either stopped by authorities or executed improperly by the terrorists themselves. According to a 2013 report on Muslim-American terrorism by the Triangle Center on Terrorism and Homeland Security, Muslim-American terrorism has claimed only thirty-seven lives in the United States from 9/11 through 2013. Over the same period, there were more than 190,000 murders in the United States. Before the Boston Marathon bombing, there had been no successful bomb plots by jihadist extremists in the United States since 9/11.

Despite the attention paid to homegrown Islamic extremists, other extremist groups have been more likely to commit violent acts. According a 2011 study released by the New America Foundation, right-wing extremists killed more people than Islamic jihadists between 9/11 and 2011. Non-jihadists were also more likely to obtain the components for making a bomb. In addition, the study reported that none of the jihadist attacks used weapons of mass destruction—commonly defined as chemical, biological, or radiological weapons. "In the aftermath of the 9/11 attacks, one of the fears of ordinary citizens and terrorism experts alike was that a new wave of terrorists would strike, some of them armed with chemical, biological, radiological or even nuclear materials," write the study's authors:

> Ten years later, we have yet to see an Islamist terrorist incident involving such weapons in the United States, and no Islamist militant in this country has made a documented attempt to even acquire such devices. Yet this is not the case for other terrorists. Indeed, the record of the past decade suggests that if a chemical, biological or radiological attack were to take place in the United States,

it is more likely that it would come not from an Islamist terrorist but from a right-wing extremist or anarchist.[29]

Focusing resources on homegrown Islamic terror threats could lessen attention to more dangerous sources of domestic terrorism.

Local Partners

The Muslim-American community has a key role in preventing homegrown Islamic terrorism. Community leaders are working to promote mainstream Islamic thinking, especially with younger Muslim-Americans, to offset the extremist propaganda they may encounter. "We do believe there's an element targeting our youth and our communities," says Muslim religious leader Mohamed Hagmagid Ali, president of the Islamic Society of North America. "But we are saying Muslims are really engaged in this fight."[30]

The efforts of the Muslim community to prevent domestic terrorism have been successful in many cases. According to Peter Bergen, a CNN national security analyst, in more than 20 percent of post-9/11 Islamist terror cases in the United States, law enforcement organizations received tips from the Muslim community or cooperation from family members of the alleged plotters. "Leaders of the Muslim community and the Muslim community itself have contributed significantly to the resolution of many of the things that we have resolved over the course of the last 12 to 18 months," said U.S. Attorney General Eric Holder in 2011. "Tips that we have received, information that has been shared, has been critical to our efforts to disrupting plots that otherwise might have occurred."[31]

In 2009, five men from the Washington, D.C., area were detained in Pakistan, where they had been trying to join the fight against U.S. forces in Afghanistan. The families of the men had become suspicious that the men had traveled overseas to perform acts of terrorism. The families approached the Council on American-Islamic Relations (CAIR), which encouraged them to make contact with the FBI with their information.

Five American men accused of joining the fight against U.S. forces in Afghanistan are moved to a prison by Pakistani police officers in January 2010.

Law enforcement is taking the threat of homegrown Islamic extremists seriously, but they need help from everyone in the community. In order to prevent a domestic terror attack, everyone in the community, from law enforcement to local religious groups, must help fight domestic terrorism at its roots. "The best way to prevent violent extremism is to work with the Muslim American community—which has consistently rejected terrorism—to identify signs of radicalization and partner with law enforcement when an individual is drifting towards violence," says President Barack Obama. "And these partnerships can only work when we recognize that Muslims are a fundamental part of the American family."[32]

CHAPTER 3

ECO-TERRORISM

For Rebecca Rubin, a love of animals began at an early age. Born in April 1973 in British Columbia, Canada, to a Canadian mother and an American father, Rubin loved books about threatened or abused animals and as a young girl dreamed of becoming a veterinarian. In college, Rubin became involved with groups focused on protecting wildlife and the environment. She participated in peaceful protests for several groups, including a hunger strike.

In 1997, Rubin moved in with David Barbarash, an animal rights activist she had met a few years earlier while protesting the development of a peat bog near Vancouver. Barbarash had previous run-ins with the law and had served a jail sentence for releasing cats from a lab at the University of Alberta and causing $50,000 in property damage. Around this time, Rubin crossed the line from animal rights activist to violent extremist.

With Barbarash, Rubin joined one of the most notorious groups of eco-terrorists in the United States. Called "The Family" by law enforcement, the group was accused of twenty acts of arson between 1996 and 2001 in five Western states. Members operated on behalf of the extremist organizations the Earth Liberation Front (ELF) and the Animal Liberation Front (ALF). According to a grand jury indictment, the group sought to "influence and affect the conduct of government, private business and the civilian population through force, violence, sabotage, mass destruction, intimidation, and coercion, and to retaliate against government and private businesses by similar means."[33]

The remains of a restaurant in Vail, Colorado, continue to smolder a day after an arson attack by Rebecca Rubin and "The Family," an eco-terrorist group. The group was accused of twenty acts of arson between 1996 and 2001 in five Western states.

In 1997, Rubin participated in her first arson with The Family. She assembled firebombs to attack the U.S. Bureau of Land Management wild horse facility in Burns, Oregon, where some horses were scheduled to be slaughtered. The resulting fire destroyed the facility. In a 1998 attack, Rubin and The Family targeted a Vail, Colorado, ski resort they believed was encroaching on a lynx habitat. They carried backpacks filled with fuel containers up a steep, snowy mountain and buried them in the snow. A few days later, members of the group returned to the ski resort and set the fires. The fires caused property damage and revenue loss of $24.5 million.

At the time, the group's tactics and attacks were popular with many in the environmental and animal rights movements who were frustrated by the slow pace of change. "There was a lot of energy and excitement and support for it," says Leslie James Pickering, a former ELF spokesperson. "People really felt like, 'If we don't like what's going on and we ask (government and companies) to stop politely and they don't, we have another recourse.'"[34]

To catch the eco-terrorists, the FBI and state police forces set up a task force called Operation Backfire. After years of gathering evidence against the group, the police began making arrests in December 2005. In 2006, the U.S. Attorney General and the FBI announced an indictment against eleven former members of the group, including Rubin, and called them terrorists. Faced with a substantial prison sentence, Rubin went into hiding in Canada.

In 2012, Rubin surrendered to the FBI. She was sentenced to five years in prison in January 2014. At her sentencing, Rubin expressed remorse for her actions. "I was so convinced at the righteousness of my beliefs, that I chose to ignore my own wrongdoing,"[35] she said. In a letter to the judge, Rubin apologized. "Although at the time I believed my only motivation was my deep love for the earth, I now understand that impatience, anger, egotism and self-righteousness were also involved," she wrote. "In retrospect, I recognize how immature my actions were. I am now forty years old and have had much time to reflect on and consider the consequences of my choices, and my thinking has become much more coherent. I know now that my actions were not merely destructive of inanimate objects but were also harmful to other, feeling human beings."[36]

The Rise of Eco-Terrorism

Since the 1970s, many groups have advocated for more stringent legal protection and regulation for animals and the environment. Some activists have become frustrated with the slow pace of change and legislation. A few have turned to violence against the companies, individuals, and practices that they believe are abusive to animals and the environment.

Eco-terrorism is defined as acts of violence committed in support of ecological, environmental, or animal rights causes against individuals or their property. In support of these causes, radical groups have targeted automobile dealerships, housing developments, forestry companies, medical research laboratories, restaurants, fur farms, and other industries across the country.

Although Islamic terrorist threats have generally received more attention from the public, eco-terrorism is one of the country's most active terrorist movements. Since the 1970s, radical en-

Animal Enterprise Terrorism Act

In 2006, the Animal Enterprise Terrorism Act (AETA) was signed into law. It expands the federal government's authority over animal rights extremists who participate in criminal activity. The law prohibits any person from engaging in conduct for the purpose of damaging or interfering with the operations of an animal enterprise. The law covers any action that either causes damages or the loss of real or personal property or that places a person in reasonable fear of injury. The law gave law enforcement more authority to target animal rights activists.

Member of the pharmaceutical industry applauded the law's passage, saying that it would provide protection for the biomedical research community and their families against intimidation and harassment from animal rights extremists. Several animal rights and civil liberties groups, however, opposed the law's passage. Camille Hankins, a representative of Win Animal Rights, said the law violated Americans' First Amendment rights to free speech and assembly. "It's overly broad, overly vague and restricts freedom of speech and freedom of assembly," she said. In 2013, a lawsuit challenging the constitutionality of the law was dismissed in a U.S. district court.

Quoted in Steve Mitchell. "Analysis: Bill targets animal activists." UPI, November 14, 2006. www.upi.com /Health_News/2006/11/14/Analysis-Bill-targets-animal -activists/UPI-50481163555788.

vironmental and animal rights groups have taken responsibility for hundreds of violent acts and crimes, including bombings, vandalism, harassment, and arson. According to the Anti-Defamation League, a civil rights and human relations organization, these crimes have caused more than $175 million in damage.

Two of the most well-known organizations that aim to unite activists for animal rights and the environment are the Animal Liberation Front (ALF) and the Earth Liberation Front (ELF). Eco-terrorists that operate on behalf of these organizations and others usually work in small, autonomous cells. They travel from place to place and are usually very difficult to infiltrate, identify, or stop. An activist can become a member of an eco-terrorist group simply by carrying out an illegal action that supports its cause. Extremists tend to join the groups through personal contacts and work in small cells or groups of like-minded members. Eco-terrorists associated with these groups are often difficult for law enforcement to identify.

Animal Liberation Front

The Animal Liberation Front (ALF) is the country's most active and extreme animal rights movement. Its members oppose any form of animal experimentation and mistreatment. Members aim to rescue animals from places of abuse. In some cases, they use vandalism, arson, and other attacks to cause economic damage to those companies and individuals who profit from the exploitation of animals. ALF members have claimed responsibility for hundreds of crimes, including animal releases and property destruction.

In July 2009, the home and three vehicles belonging to Michael Selsted, a pathologist at the University of California, Irvine, were vandalized with paint and paint stripper. Vandals also spray-painted the word "killer" on Selsted's garage door. ALF claimed responsibility for the vandalism. They targeted Selsted because they were unhappy with the animal research his lab

A mink research lab at Michigan State University lies in ruins following a bombing in 1992 by the Animal Liberation Front, which opposes human exploitation of animals.

Protesters proclaiming to support the Earth Liberation Front march in Portland, Oregon, in 2002.

conducted. An ALF statement said, "We can only hope that one day someone will make you suffer as much as the animals in the laboratories you work in."[37]

Earth Liberation Front

Modeled after ALF, Earth Liberation Front (ELF) is made up of autonomous groups of people whose common goal is to cause economic damage for entities and individuals who profit from the destruction and exploitation of the environment. Many ELF supporters see the actions of its extremists as similar to those of the Boston Tea Party, when revolutionaries destroyed property to draw public attention to an important issue. Like ALF, ELF is not a centralized group, but instead considers itself to be a leaderless resistance structure. Individual cells are linked by shared beliefs and ideology. To join ELF, activists form a cell and launch a direct action against a target that opposes the group's values. Once a cell's action is complete, it may dissolve or plan another action.

ELF has claimed responsibility for hundreds of crimes in the name of environmental protection. In particular, ELF members have battled against urban sprawl. They believe development is a harmful and unnecessary encroachment on natural habitats.

To protest development of natural lands, arsonists burned down a San Diego housing complex under construction in 2003, causing property damage around $50 million. At the scene, ELF left a 12-foot-long (3.65m) banner with the movement's acronym and a threat to burn anything built on the site. To protest the environmental damage caused by cars and sport utility vehicles, ELF members have also targeted car dealerships. In several instances, members have set fire to dealerships and burned cars and SUVs.

Significant Damage

According to FBI estimates, members of these two eco-terrorist groups have committed more than six hundred criminal acts since 1996. The terrorist actions have resulted in more than $43 million in damages. Two of the main terror tactics used by these groups are arson and bombings. According to a 2013 study by the National Consortium for the Study of Terrorism and Responses to Terrorism (START), between 1995 and 2010 there were 239 arsons and bombings committed by the two groups. A little more than half (55 percent) were attributed to ELF members, with 45 percent attributed to ALF members. Other tactics used by these groups to inflict damage and spread terror include tree spiking, vandalism, intimidation and harassment, and animal release.

Although they have caused millions of dollars in property and economic damage, representatives of ALF and ELF object to being called terrorists. They point out that their members have not killed anyone with their violence to date. Critics of the groups' tactics say violence against property is still dangerous. As the violence of eco-terrorist attacks increases, many believe it is only a matter of time before a human life is lost. "Animal and environmental rights extremists pose a threat to American public safety," write the START study's authors. "Domestic terrorism attacks outnumber international ones seven to one in the United States and animal and environmental rights extremists compose a dangerous segment of domestic extremist movements."[38]

TYPES OF TARGETS ATTACKED BY ECO-TERRORISTS, 1995–2010

According to the National Consortium for the Study of Terrorism and Responses to Terrorism, 239 arsons and bombings were committed by the Earth Liberation Front (ELF) and Animal Liberation Front (ALF) between 1995 and 2010. The attacks targeted a variety of public and private places.

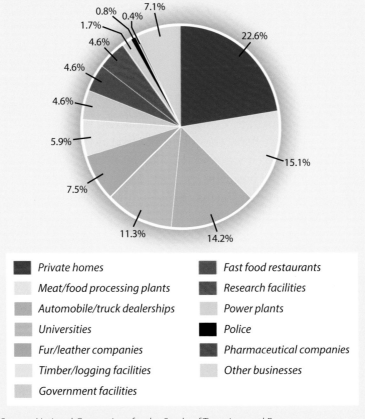

■ Private homes		■ Fast food restaurants
Meat/food processing plants		Research facilities
Automobile/truck dealerships		Power plants
Universities		Police
Fur/leather companies		Pharmaceutical companies
Timber/logging facilities		Other businesses
Government facilities		

Source: National Consortium for the Study of Terrorism and Responses to Terrorism. *An Overview of Bombing and Arson Attacks by Environmental and Animal Rights Extremists in the United States, 1995–2010*, May 2013, p. 10. www.start.umd .edu/sites/default/files/files/publications/START_BombingAndArsonAttacksBy EnvironmentalAndAnimalRightsExtremists_May2013.pdf.

Arson Attacks

As a member of ELF, Daniel McGowan participated in two arsons in Oregon in 2001, causing millions of dollars in damage. The targets were Superior Lumber, a timber company that engaged in old-growth logging, and Jefferson Poplar tree farm, which McGowan incorrectly believed was participating in genetic engineering projects. "I had severe reservations about being involved in destroying property, but I felt very strongly about the issues," McGowan said in a 2007 interview:

> I felt at the time, we were not getting anywhere with sort of polite protests, very disenchanted with the whole political process. And we targeted these two facilities for um, you know, using fire, and destroyed a significant portion of them. The actions were intended to destroy corporate property. We took extreme precautions in these actions so we wouldn't harm anyone. But after the second arson, I became incredibly disenchanted with the use of fire. I saw the rebound effect; I thought about how dangerous it was and the life, the lives that we put at risk by igniting basically a million and a half-dollar arson at Jefferson Poplar Farms. Along with some other issues

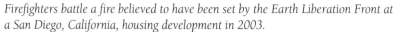

Firefighters battle a fire believed to have been set by the Earth Liberation Front at a San Diego, California, housing development in 2003.

it just led to me leaving the group and moving on with life, getting back to the activism that I had been involved with for the last ten years.[39]

In December 2005, McGowan was arrested by the FBI as part of Operation Backfire, a sting designed to round up extreme environmental activists.

COUNTERPRODUCTIVE TACTICS

"My personal view is that the ELF has done more harm than good. I am sympathetic to much of their view of the world, but their tactics are counterproductive and often extremely dangerous."—Rik Scarce, author of *Eco-Warriors: Understanding the Radical Environmental Movement*.

Quoted in "Interview: Rik Scarce, Author of 'Eco-Warriors.'" PBS.org, September 13, 2011. www.pbs.org/pov/ifatreefalls/eco-warriors-rik-scarce-interview.php.

At his trial, McGowan pled guilty to conspiracy and arson charges. The judge in his case sentenced McGowan to seven years in prison and applied the terrorism enhancement to his sentencing. Enacted in 1995 after the bombings of the World Trade Center and the Alfred P. Murrah Federal Building in Oklahoma City, the terrorism enhancement is a measure that allows judges to increase a defendant's sentence if his or her offense involves or intends to promote a federal crime of terrorism. In recent years, the USA PATRIOT Act (Uniting and Strengthening America by Providing Appropriate Tools Required to Intercept and Obstruct Terrorism Act of 2001) and other legislation has allowed judges to apply antiterrorism laws and punishments to radical environmental and animal rights extremists. At McGowan's sentencing, the prosecution claimed that the arsons by ELF and ALF were similar to racially motivated terroristic acts committed by the Ku Klux Klan.

The judge ruled that McGowan set the fire at the tree farm to intimidate the state government and influence the government's conduct through intimidation or coercion. By finding the crime met this legal standard, the judge was allowed to consider

Daniel McGowan sits in front of his home in Brooklyn, New York, in 2006. He was sentenced to seven years in prison for arson attacks committed with the Earth Liberation Front.

increasing McGowan's prison sentence to life. Eventually, the judge decided to sentence him to only seven years in jail, partly because McGowan had persuaded others who were involved in the arsons to plead guilty.

Are Tactics Effective?

A debate exists over whether the destructive actions of eco-terrorism have been effective. While arsons and property damage have a short-term effect, over the long term little has changed in many cases. Condominiums, housing developments, and ski resorts have been rebuilt. New sport utility vehicles continue to be manufactured by auto companies and driven by Americans. Scientists at targeted labs re-create and continue genetic experimentation. In fact, the rebuilding of destroyed property may end up damaging the environment even more. "In some senses, the destruction has been done twice-over: twice the trees were cut for the 2 x 4s to build those burned buildings and twice the metals were mined for the SUVs,"[40] says Rik Scarce, author of *Eco-Warriors: Understanding the Radical Environmental Movement.*

In addition, the real damage may have been in the battle for public sympathies. By resorting to violence, animal rights and environmental activists may have made it more difficult to achieve their ultimate goals of protecting animals and the envi-

Eco-Attack on GMOs

In 2013, about one hundred genetically modified papaya trees were cut down with machetes on Hawaii's Big Island. Officials believe the destruction was an act of eco-terrorism. The majority of Hawaiian papaya from the state's $11 million papaya industry is grown from genetically modified seeds that are resistant to a ring spot virus that devastated the island's papaya crop in the 1950s. The 2013 attack resulted in damages of approximately $3,000. In prior years, similar attacks caused more damage, with about ten acres of papaya trees being cut down in 2011 and about 8,500 trees cut down in 2010. After the 2011 incident, Delan Perry, vice president of the Hawaii Papaya Industry Association, said, "It's hard to imagine anybody putting that much effort into doing something like that. It means somebody has to have [a] passionate reason."

Quoted in Jennifer Sinco Kelleher. "Genetically Modified Papayas Attacked in Hawaii." *Huffington Post*, August 20, 2011. www.huffingtonpost.com/2011/08/20/genetically-modified-papayas-attacked_n_932152.html.

ronment. "There is no greater stigma in our society than that of 'terrorist.' No one listens to terrorists. Their arguments fall on deaf ears. They are imprisoned, as Daniel McGowan is, under extreme conditions reminiscent of the terrorism suspects at Guantanamo," says Scarce. "So the ELF's penchant for destruction—never mind that no human life has ever been lost as a result of their actions—allows it to be painted as a terrorist group."[41]

Activism vs. Terrorism

For some, McGowan's actions and the actions of other extreme animal rights and environmental activists are a form of activism and should not be compared to terrorism. "You use such a serious word for something that doesn't live up to most people's expectations of that word, it really diminishes the power and the importance of the word,"[42] says Lauren Regan, a member of McGowan's legal team and executive director of the Eugene, Oregon-based Civil Liberties Defense Center, which provides legal protection to environmental and social justice activists from corporate and governmental attacks on civil liberties.

Some object to the terrorist label because the environmental and animal rights groups typically target property with their actions, not human life. In fact, no person has ever been hurt to date in an ELF or ALF arson. McGowan and his sister agree the arsons and property damage inflicted by extreme activists should not be called terrorism. McGowan says he believes the word "terrorism" has become something people use to win a public relations battle and that law enforcement uses the label to get more funding and attention from the media. His sister, who lives in New York City and experienced the devastation of 9/11 firsthand, says there is no comparison between the actions of al Qaeda, which harmed thousands of people, and the actions of her brother, which physically harmed no one.

ENVIRONMENTAL ACTIVISM UNDER ATTACK

"The courts have been used to push the limits of what constitutes 'terrorism,' and to hit activists with disproportionate penalties and prison sentences. In this realm the word terrorist is used early, and used often, to skew public opinion against defendants before they ever set foot in a courtroom."—Will Potter, journalist and author of *Green Is the New Red: An Insider's Account of a Social Movement Under Siege*

Quoted in Robert Jensen. "Green is the New Red: Environmental Activists Under Attack." Grist.org, July 26, 2011. http://grist.org/politics/2011-07-26-green-is-the-new-red-environmental-activists-under-attack.

Will Potter, a journalist and environmental activist, says he believes the label of terrorist was deliberately created by the targeted corporations to turn the public against environmental activists. "This was actually created by the industries that are being protested," he explains:

In the mid-1980s, these corporations got together and created a new word called "eco-terrorist"—because at the time, these protest movements were growing very quickly and effectively, and they had widespread public support. There clearly was a concern that unless public opinion shifted, there'd be a really big problem on their hands. So they made up this new word, and then started using public relations campaigns, lobbying, and held congressional hearings. Eventually, that language changed the popular discourse of how we talk about protest. And it was incredibly effective, to the point that now not only does the FBI label animal rights and environmentalists as the number-one domestic terrorism threat—even though they've never harmed a single human being—but we have new legislation that singles these protesters out for felonies and as terrorists for what are, in some cases, nonviolent protests.[43]

Others in law enforcement disagree and support extreme activists' crimes being labeled, investigated, prosecuted, and punished as terrorist acts. When the U.S. Office of Inspector General proposed in 2003 that eco-terrorism cases be moved from the FBI's counterterrorism unit to the criminal investigative division, the FBI declined. The Bureau explained the counterterrorism unit was best able to handle these types of cases because ELF, ALF, and similar extreme groups are organized the same way as terrorist cells.

Regardless of whether or not they are injured, victims of an eco-attack feel terrorized. "You don't have to be Bonnie and Clyde to be a bank robber, and you don't have to be Al Qaeda to be a terrorist,"[44] says one prosecutor. Assistant United States Attorney Stephen F. Peifer, one of the prosecutors in McGowan's case, agrees and says that McGowan is a classic example of someone who gradually increased his radicalism over time. Peifer says, "If you use violence or the threat of violence to further your ideological goals, you're guilty of terrorism."[45]

CHAPTER 4

DOMESTIC TERROR ONLINE

In August 2012, forty-year-old Wade Michael Page opened fire on strangers at a Sikh temple in Oak Creek, Wisconsin. Carrying a 9mm handgun and multiple magazines of ammunition, he fatally shot six people and wounded four others before shooting himself in the head. With turbans and long beards, Sikhs are often mistaken for Muslims and have sometimes become targets of anti-Muslim bias in the United States. The FBI labeled the shooting as an act of domestic terrorism.

Investigators looking into Page's background discovered that he was a U.S. army veteran who was deeply involved in the white supremacist culture. In the months leading up to the shooting, Page had used the Internet to grow increasingly radical. The Internet connected Page to others who shared his extremist beliefs. He spent much of his time online, hanging out on websites and forums with others who held similar views. He was an active participant in an online message forum for a white supremacist group and joined in dozens of conversations. He was also active on social media, with at least two Facebook pages under the names "Wade Hammer" and "Jackboot." While online, Page urged others to act on their beliefs. "If you are wanting to meet people, get involved and become active," he wrote in one post. "Stop hiding behind the computer or making excuses."[46]

Many experts are not surprised that violent extremists like Page are using the Internet to promote their beliefs. The introduction of the World Wide Web in 1991 provided a new platform for people to share thoughts and information. On the Internet, people can create and share documents and web pages for others to read. In addition, the emergence of social media has allowed people around the world to interact, share thoughts, and discuss ideas and information. Using this technology, extremist groups can spread their message far and wide. During a May 2013 speech, President Barack Obama warned that the Internet was fueling an increase in domestic terrorism. "[T]his threat is not new," Obama said. "But technology and the Internet increase its frequency and lethality." He said that materials on the Internet could influence some people to commit terrorist acts. "Today, a person can consume hateful propaganda, commit themselves to a violent agenda and learn how to kill without leaving their home."[47]

Visitors look at a memorial near the entrance of the Sikh Temple of Wisconsin in 2013. Wade Michael Page shot and killed six temple members and himself in 2012, after using the Internet to grow increasingly radical.

Spreading a Violent Message

Violent extremists have embraced the Internet and social media. They use it to spread their message to a national and global audience. Online, extremists publicize their causes, generate political support, and recruit new followers. According to researchers with the Bipartisan Policy Center's Homeland Security Project:

> The Internet has revolutionized the way all of us communicate and do business. Its benefits to people everywhere have been enormous and will continue to drive progress in practically every area of life. At the same time, it should be recognized that, while being a force for good, the Internet has also come to play an important—and, in many ways, unique—role in radicalizing homegrown and domestic terrorists. Supporters of al Qaeda, Sovereign Citizens, white supremacists and neo-Nazis, environmental and animal liberationists, and other violent extremist groups all have embraced the Internet with great enthusiasm and vigor. They are using it as a platform to spread their ideas, connect with each other, make new recruits, and incite illegal and violent actions.[48]

Before the Internet, extremists often worked alone. It was difficult to connect with others who shared their views and ideology. Today, extremist groups use a variety of platforms and media to reach people online. On websites, extremists share unfiltered news, ideological texts, announcements, and other information. Some sites share the stories of leaders, prisoners, fallen fighters, and martyrs. Many groups also have online forums, where people meet, bond, and talk with each other about controversial issues without the fear of retribution.

Encrypted e-mail allows extremists to communicate directly and privately with each other. Encryption converts text using a secret code, making it unreadable to anyone who does not have the ability to decode it. With encrypted e-mail, extremists can exchange ideas and develop plans without worrying about their messages being intercepted or read by others outside of the group.

Social media has opened even more avenues for violent extremists to post content on blogs, social networks, video-sharing sites, and instant messaging platforms. Using social media, they can reach a more diverse audience. "Rather than being tucked away in the darkest corners of the Internet, it became possible for people to virtually stumble into extremist propaganda on sites like YouTube, Twitter, Paltalk, Facebook, and WordPress. This enabled violent extremists and terrorists to reach more people and engage new demographics, especially women,"[49] say researchers from the Bipartisan Policy Center's Homeland Security Project.

EMBRACING SOCIAL MEDIA

"It is operationally imperative that law enforcement leaders embrace the existence of social media platforms and understand how they are used by extremists as a vehicle to deliver their subversive messages."—Rob Finch and Kory Flowers, detectives in the Greensboro, North Carolina police department's Criminal Intelligence Squad

Rob Finch and Kory Flowers. "Violent Domestic Extremism and the Role of Social Media Within Law Enforcement." *The Police Chief*, vol. 80, June 2013, pp. 32–34. www.policechiefmagazine.org/magazine/index.cfm?fuseaction=display_arch&article_id=2952&issue_id=62013.

Anwar al-Awlaki, a U.S.-born cleric, was an expert at promoting Islamic extremism online. As an imam at the Dar al-Hijrah mosque in Falls Church, Virginia, Awlaki posted his sermons in English on YouTube and other websites. He operated his own blog and was active on several social networking sites. His engaging style and stirring lectures gathered a growing group of loyal Internet followers. While some of Awlaki's lectures online were nonviolent, others strongly encouraged violence. In a sermon called "44 Ways to Support Jihad," Awlaki encouraged followers to participate in suicide missions against the West and

Anwar al-Awlaki, a radical Yemeni-American cleric, gives a speech in a video released in 2010.

to sponsor families of suicide bombers. Awlaki engaged in multiple e-mails with Major Nidal Hasan, who was arrested for the Fort Hood massacre in 2009. Awlaki encouraged his followers to set up their own social networking pages, establish discussion forums, send e-mail blasts, post jihadist literature, and set up websites to share information. "The internet has become a great medium for spreading the call of jihad,"[50] Awlaki wrote.

Online Radicalization

For many would-be terrorists, the Internet is a place to start. People no longer have to be exposed to violent and extreme ideas in person in order to become radicalized. Instead, they can find everything they need with the click of a mouse.

The Internet connects people with similar interests across great distances, which makes it easier for people to meet other extremists and connect with extreme groups, even if they have no real-life contact with these groups. Gordon Lederman, former chief counsel for national security and investigations of the U.S. Senate Homeland Security and Governmental Affairs Committee, said:

> The Internet has facilitated radicalization to violent Islamist extremism and resulting terrorist activity. . . . [V]iolent Islamist extremists originally used password-protected forums, but they are now present on mainstream sites such as YouTube. The Internet enables individuals who are vulnerable to radicalization to find

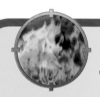

Threats on Social Media

In 2013, a sixteen-year-old teen from Detroit, Michigan, was arrested and charged with domestic terrorism, a felony that is punishable by up to twenty years in jail, after he made an online threat against the Orchard Lake St. Mary's Polish Country Fair, a school fundraising event. The teen, who had been linked to local gangs, posted the threat on the social media sites Instagram and Twitter. The threatening posts included several photos showing a handgun, an assault rifle, and several fully loaded high-capacity magazines for the handgun. Parents of a student at Orchard Lake St. Mary's notified local police about the online threat. After being questioned by law enforcement, the teen admitted to making the threat on Twitter.

Mike McDaniel, an associate professor at Cooley Law School and director of the school's homeland security law program, disagrees with charging the teen with domestic terrorism. "You don't want to cheapen the definition of terrorism," says McDaniel. "The idea of terrorism is that the threat of violence is to compel or coerce intimidation with a political or social objective in mind. In my mind, it's not terrorism."

Quoted in John Turk. "Law Professor Objects to Terrorist Charge for Teen After Threats to Orchard Lake St. Mary's Polish County Fair." *Oakland Press*, May 29, 2013. www.theoaklandpress.com/general-news/20130529/law-professor-objects-to-terrorist-charge-for-teen-after-threats-to-orchard-lake-st-marys-polish-county-fair.

violent Islamist extremist material easily and to self-segregate and interact only with individuals who share that ideology—and in the privacy of their own homes.[51]

While there is no single type of material that causes a person to carry out violent terror acts, the Internet's ability to immerse individuals in extreme content for an extended period of time is a factor in many cases where individuals have become radicalized. According to social psychologist Tom Pyszczynski, when an individual is repeatedly exposed to material about martyrdom and death, combined with videos of suicide missions and beheadings, it can result in an overpowering sense of the individual's own mortality. Pyszczynski says this increases the individual's support for suicide missions and other brutal terroristic methods. According to terrorism analyst Marc Sageman, videos from conflict zones that show atrocities by Western troops can trigger outrage that motivates an individual to action.

Social media is another powerful tool in radicalization. In online forums, chat rooms, or other social media sites, people interact with others who share the same views. Without the presence of moderate viewpoints, participants begin to think of extreme ideas and behaviors as normal. According to Elizabeth Englander, director of the Massachusetts Aggression Reduction Center:

> Without the Internet . . . you might have a few people in a community with a very extremist view, but there wouldn't be anybody else who shared their view. They might come to the conclusion that these extremist views are wrong or incorrect or kooky. With the Internet, they can always find others who share their views. Suddenly there is [a] community that says, "You're not crazy, you're right." That's very powerful.[52]

In addition, the anonymous nature of the Internet allows people to become bolder, believing that they can hide their true identities. With reduced inhibitions, individuals and groups can

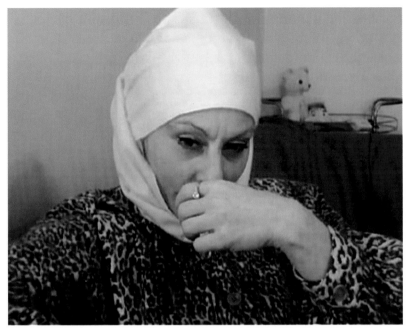

Colleen R. LaRose, an American woman known as "Jihad Jane," is seen in an undated image released in 2010 from a website believed to be maintained by the terror suspect.

become more hostile, extreme, and aggressive online. Eventually this hostile and aggressive attitude and behavior may bleed into offline behavior and activities.

In 2008, Colleen LaRose, an American from a small town in Pennsylvania, became involved in online extremism. In Pennsylvania, LaRose had few offline contacts who shared her views. She turned to the Internet and frequented jihadist websites and extremist forums. She started commenting on YouTube videos about conflicts in the Middle East under the name "Jihad Jane." On social networking sites, she said she wanted to help suffering Muslims. She posted videos online of attacks by U.S. troops in Iraq. Eventually, she began to use the Internet to recruit radicals and materials to support violent jihad missions. In October 2009, the FBI arrested LaRose for her involvement in a plot to kill a Swedish cartoonist who had offended some Muslims with a drawing of the Prophet Muhammad. "LaRose showed that you can become a terrorist in the comfort of your own bedroom," says Bruce Hoffman, professor of security studies at Georgetown University. "You couldn't do that 10 years ago."[53]

Restricting Extremist Sites

A debate has emerged over how to handle websites, social networks, and other Internet sites that promote and display extremist ideals, threats, and propaganda. Some people believe the government should take a stronger role in cracking down on

Holocaust Museum Shooting

In June 2009, eighty-eight-year-old James von Brunn walked into the United States Holocaust Memorial Museum, one of Washington D.C.'s most visited sites, and began shooting without warning. As tourists scrambled for cover, von Brunn fatally shot a security guard before he was shot himself.

Von Brunn was a white supremacist who supported various conspiracy theories about Jews, blacks, and other minority groups. He also had a long-running distrust and hatred of the federal government. He had served more than six years in prison in the 1980s for a failed attempt to kidnap Federal Reserve board members. In recent years, von Brunn used the Internet to spread his extremist views. He was active on right-wing extremist message boards, posting anti-government and anti-Semitic messages.

Von Brunn also set up a website called The Holy Western Empire where he posted anti-Semitic content. Officials said they had been watching von Brunn's online postings and his website had been listed as a hate site. "We've been tracking this guy for decades," said Heidi Beirich, director of research for the Southern Poverty Law Center's Intelligence Project, which tracks hate crimes. "He thinks the Jews control the Federal Reserve, the banking system, that basically all Jews are evil." After the shooting, some of von Brunn's online writings were deleted from many websites. While awaiting trial for the security guard's murder, von Brunn died in 2010.

Quoted in "Von Brunn Charged in Holocaust Museum Slay." CBS News.com, June 11, 2009. www.cbsnews.com/news/von-brunn-charged-in-holocaust-museum-slay.

these sites and shutting them down. If the sites and posts are not available online, it will make it more difficult for extremists to communicate and groom new recruits. In the United Kingdom, Prime Minister David Cameron announced in November 2013 that he wanted to expand Internet censorship to block extremist websites. "We have had repeated meetings of the extremism task force . . . setting out a whole series of steps that we will take to counter the extremist narrative, including by blocking online sites. . . . We will take all these steps and many more to keep our country safe,"[54] said Cameron.

Shutting down an extremist website, however, is not as simple as it sounds. Once a site is shut down, extremists can easily reopen it under a new name and web address. On the new site, they can continue promoting the same beliefs and propaganda. To keep up with the ever-changing nature of the Internet, law enforcement would need to use significant resources to shut down each extremist website, spending valuable resources that may be better used in other areas.

Online Extremism vs. Free Speech

Limiting Internet communications is considered by some people to be a blow to individual freedoms. Banning certain websites and Internet content is often in direct conflict with the constitutional right of freedom of speech. In the United States, the First Amendment to the Constitution guarantees the right of freedom of speech to all Americans, even if their opinions and words are offensive to others. "The United States is perhaps the only country in the world that allows for protection of hate speech. Much of this has to do with the idea that a free exchange of ideas is important and that allowing speech—even hate-filled speech— can be a safety valve that helps prevent outbreaks of violence,"[55] says Edward J. Eberle, professor at the Roger Williams University School of Law.

In 1997, the U.S. Supreme Court ruled in *Reno v. ACLU* that the First Amendment protections for freedom of speech extended to the Internet, saying that speech on the Internet should

Chris Hansen, the lead attorney for the ACLU, announces their legal victory at the U.S. Supreme Court in 1997 in New York City. The court ruled that First Amendment protections extend to the Internet.

receive the highest level of First Amendment protection. In the case of violent extremism, the desire to make it harder for radical extremists to communicate, share information, and spread propaganda, no matter how offensive, needs to be balanced against First Amendment rights. According to Phyllis Gerstenfeld, professor and chairman of the criminal justice department at California State University, Stanislaus:

> It is often difficult to balance the protection of civil liberties, especially freedom of expression, with the desire to avoid bloodshed. Those charged with enforcing the laws have sometimes overstepped the bounds of their authority—and have infringed upon First Amendment rights—when they have attempted to investigate or silence extremists.[56]

For some people, no amount of censorship online is acceptable, even when done in the name of domestic security. Gary Shapiro is the president and CEO of the Consumer Electronics Association and believes the government should not censor speech on the Internet. He says keeping the Internet uncensored is important to preserving the right to freedom of speech in the United States and warns of legislation to censor Internet speech. "The main intention behind each of these bills may be good . . . but they all give government far too much control over what can and cannot be said online, opening the door to greater restrictions. Censorship is not the way to fight piracy or protect against threats to security or privacy,"[57] says Shapiro.

DIFFICULT TO FIND REAL THREATS

"Social media generates so much 'stuff' and there are so many people involved in chatting with radicals on the internet . . . and no intelligence service has completely figured out how to separate the 'chatter' from the 'real,' significant stuff."—Peter Neumann, professor at King's College London

Quoted in Dan Rivers. "How Terror Can Breed Through Social Media." CNN.com, April 28, 2013. www.cnn.com/2013/04/27/world/rivers-social-media-terror.

Using the Internet for Intelligence

Law enforcement and U.S. intelligence agencies have joined extremists online, using their digital operations against them. Monitoring extremist activity online can be an important source of information for investigators working to prevent domestic terrorism. Agents can monitor online activity and communications to understand how domestic terrorists work through the Internet. They can scour websites, forums, and social media to gather information, track, and disrupt domestic terror plots. "This information can be used to gain strategic intelligence on terrorist groups' intentions and networks, on tactical intelligence on terrorist operations and the people who are involved in them, and on evidence that can be used in prosecutions,"[58] say researchers at the Bipartisan Policy Center. In fact, shutting down extremist websites, chat rooms, and forums may take away a valuable source of information.

The Armed Forces Career Center in Catonsville, Maryland, was the site of an Internet sting operation by the FBI against jihadist Antonio Martinez in December 2010.

Social media can provide investigators with a wealth of information about a suspect's likelihood of engaging in a terrorist act. Investigators monitor a suspect's social media sites. Over time, investigators may notice that a suspect's daily posts are becoming more violent and action-oriented. If needed, they can intervene to prevent a successful terroristic act. In September 2010, the FBI successfully intervened and prevented Justin Moose, an anti-abortion extremist, from bombing an abortion clinic. Law enforcement had started monitoring Moose after receiving a tip regarding Moose's Facebook page, where he had posted recipes for manufacturing explosives and posts about the justified murder of abortion doctors. Agents arrested Moose after he attempted to provide explosives to an undercover federal agent.

In December 2010, Antonio Martinez, a twenty-five-year-old construction worker from Baltimore, Maryland, parked a truck he thought was packed with explosives outside a military recruitment center. He planned to detonate the truck. When he pressed the button to trigger the explosion, nothing happened. Instead of an explosion, Martinez was surrounded by counter-terrorism officers and arrested. He was charged with the attempted murder of federal officers and attempted use of a weapon of mass destruction. Law enforcement used the Internet to catch Martinez, who kept a Facebook page where he posted about violent jihad. When an FBI source noted Martinez's social media profile and posts, an FBI informant contacted him. Martinez told the informant about his idea to target the recruitment station. When Martinez moved into action, FBI agents were ready. They supplied him with a truck and fake explosives. Agents were also on site to make sure the terror plot was not successful.

Keeping Up Online

As Internet use evolves, keeping up with extremists online is a challenging but critical step in the fight against domestic terrorism. Extremists bent on violence will use every tool at their disposal to further their agenda, including those online. Law enforcement must be adequately prepared to use the same digital tools, particularly social media, as they attempt to prevent and investigate acts of domestic terror. Rob Finch and Kory Flowers, detectives on the Criminal Intelligence Squad of the Greensboro, North Carolina, police department, write:

> Criminally subversive groups and extremist individuals are no longer solely meeting at a centralized location at a specific time to indoctrinate new adherents or discuss and plan acts of violence. Social media has provided a fast and effective way for extremists to disseminate their messages to a larger group of like-minded individuals . . . Law enforcement has a duty and responsibility to monitor these social media sites in hope of identifying planned criminal acts or indicators of future violent behavior.[59]

CHAPTER 5

PREVENTING DOMESTIC TERRORISM

In 2003, Gale Nettles designed a deadly plan while in a Mississippi prison. Angry with the federal government for putting him in jail for counterfeiting, Nettles planned to bomb the federal courthouse in Chicago after his release from prison. He confided in a fellow inmate about his planned attack. Instead of keeping the information quiet, the inmate reported his conversation with Nettles to the FBI office in Jackson, Mississippi. The Jackson office notified the FBI's Joint Terrorism Task Force (JTTF) in Chicago, which determined that Nettles was a real threat. When Nettles was released from prison, the JTTF placed him under surveillance.

Soon after his release, Nettles traveled to Chicago and began searching for ammonium nitrate to make a powerful fertilizer-based bomb. He contacted a supplier his prison friend had mentioned, not knowing the supplier was really an undercover FBI agent. The undercover agent agreed to sell 2,000 pounds (907kg) of nitrate to Nettles, but switched the material with a harmless substitute. Then Nettles asked his prison friend to introduce him to someone in al Qaeda or another terrorist group. He planned to sell extra explosives to these groups. In response, the JTTF set up another sting operation. An undercover agent pretended to be an international terrorist and paid Nettles ten thousand dollars for his explosives. A short time later, federal agents moved in and arrested Nettles.

The investigation that led to Nettles's arrest was a coordinated effort between many people and agencies. Over a ten-month period the investigation involved more than two hundred law enforcement officers and agents from the FBI, the JTTF, and more than twenty federal, state, and local agencies. In September 2005, Nettles was convicted of plotting to destroy a federal building and other charges. He was sentenced to life in prison. "The best part of the case was knowing that we actually prevented a terrorist attack and saved lives in the process,"[60] says Special Agent Sonjia Wing, who was one of the agents on the case.

Federal prosecutor Patrick J. Fitzgerald announces the arrest of William Nettles on charges of plotting to use a fertilizer truck bomb to blow up a federal courthouse in Chicago, Illinois.

Taking Charge: The FBI

In the United States, the FBI is the lead agency in domestic terrorism cases. FBI agents work to identify and prevent domestic terrorism acts before they occur. When an act of domestic terrorism does occur, the FBI is the lead federal agency to respond to a crisis situation and acts as an on-site manager for the federal government. In the days and weeks after the incident, the FBI leads the investigation.

Prevention is one of the FBI's overriding goals. At the same time, the agency acknowledges that balance must be struck between preventing extremist violence and protecting the civil liberties of Americans. "It's an especially tall order given the civil liberties we all enjoy as American citizens, including the right to free speech," states the FBI website:

> Hate and anger are not crimes; neither are hard-line and poisonous ideologies. It's only when actions by groups or individuals cross the line into threats, the actual use of force or violence, or other law-breaking activities that we can investigate. That goes for lone offenders, whose high degrees of autonomy make them difficult to stop before they strike. As a result, we're not shy about applying our full suite of anti-terror tools and capabilities to threats of homegrown terrorism. That includes our time-tested investigative techniques such as the use of surveillance and informants as well as the new intelligence skills and information-sharing channels we've cultivated since 9/11.[61]

The FBI works closely with many federal, state, and local agencies to prevent and investigate acts of domestic terrorism. Agencies such as the Bureau of Alcohol, Tobacco, Firearms and Explosives (ATF) and the Internal Revenue Service (IRS) play a role in preventing domestic terrorism. Along with state and local law enforcement, specialists and agents from these agencies cooperate to prevent domestic terrorism. Together, these partners gather, archive, and analyze massive amounts of information on American citizens and residents living in the United States. They follow up on leads reported by law enforcement officers and citizens about people acting suspiciously in the community.

USA PATRIOT Act

After the 9/11 attacks on the United States, U.S. Attorney General John Ashcroft presented to Congress a list of recommended changes to the law. The changes were designed to allow the country to combat terrorism more effectively. Congress quickly passed these changes, and the resulting law was named the Uniting and Strengthening America by Providing Appropriate Tools Required to Intercept and Obstruct Terrorism (USA PATRIOT) Act of 2001. The Act reduces restrictions on law enforcement's ability to investigate possible terrorist plots. It eases restrictions on searching telephone, e-mail communications, medical, financial, and other records. It also expands the definition of terrorism to include domestic terrorism. The USA PATRIOT Act defines domestic terrorism as activities within the United States that involve illegal acts dangerous to human life if the act

U.S. President George W. Bush makes the case for extending the USA PATRIOT Act at a 2004 event in Hershey, Pennsylvania.

appears to be intended to intimidate or coerce a civilian population, influence government policy through intimidation or coercion, or affect a government's actions through mass destruction, assassination, or kidnapping.

RADICAL VIEWS ARE NOT A CRIME

"In the United States, to hold radical views is not a crime . . . Only when these turn to criminal incitement and violent action or manifest intent to engage in violence is there cause for legal intervention."—Brian Michael Jenkins

Quoted in Richard Brust. "Insider Threats: Experts Try to Balance the Constitution with Law Enforcement to Find Terrorists." *ABA Journal*, July 1, 2012. www.abajournal.com /magazine/article/insider_threats_experts_try_to_balance_the_constitution_with_law _enforcemen.

On October 26, 2001, President George W. Bush signed the USA PATRIOT Act into law. "Today, we take an essential step in defeating terrorism, while protecting the constitutional rights of all Americans," he said:

> With my signature, this law will give intelligence and law enforcement officials important new tools to fight a present danger . . . We're dealing with terrorists who operate by highly sophisticated methods and technologies, some of which were not even available when our existing laws were written. The bill before me takes account of the new realities and dangers posed by modern terrorists. It will help law enforcement to identify, to dismantle, to disrupt, and to punish terrorists before they strike.[62]

Joint Terrorism Task Forces (JTTFs)

Under the USA PATRIOT Act, the Joint Terrorism Task Forces (JTTFs) were established. Led by the Justice Department and the FBI, JTTFs are the front line for preventing terrorism. There are more than one hundred JTTFs across the country. Each

Fusion Centers

State and major urban area fusion centers work along with JTTFs to prevent terrorism. While JTTFs are led by the FBI, fusion centers are owned and operated by state and local entities. These centers are the focal point within a state or local community for receipt, analysis, gathering, and sharing of intelligence between various federal, state, and local partners. The fusion centers partner with people from a variety of organizations including law enforcement, public safety, fire service, emergency responders, and public health. While the JTTFs' primary mission is to conduct investigations, the fusion centers' main purpose is to analyze information and share intelligence. When a fusion center receives a terrorism-related lead, it passes the information to a JTTF for investigation.

Fusion centers produce threat-related intelligence, which can help other law enforcement organizations in their investigations. They add state and local information to threat assessments to help federal partners like the JTTF prepare a complete national threat picture.

Fusion centers assist the FBI by providing information gathered from a variety of sources including local law enforcement and other homeland security agencies. In some cases, the FBI may consult with fusion center personnel on analyses or recommendations. The FBI may also use some fusion center personnel for analytic or investigative activities as needed.

A staffer watches the video monitors at the Palm Beach Regional Fusion Center, one of the centers operated by Homeland Security for gathering, receiving, analyzing, and sharing intelligence between various federal, state, and local agencies.

investigates acts of terrorism, develops informants, and gathers intelligence to prevent terrorist plots. The JTTFs also share FBI intelligence with outside agencies and law enforcement. A national JTTF team coordinates the FBI's work with more than forty partner agencies. It is the central point for information sharing and managing large projects that involve multiple agencies.

Each JTTF is a highly trained, locally based team of police officers, federal agents, investigators, analysts, linguists, SWAT experts, and other specialists. Members of JTTFs come from dozens of U.S. law enforcement and intelligence agencies. There are more than 4,400 law enforcement officers and agents working in JTTFs across the country.

Undercover Stings

Undercover operations and the use of informants are important tactics used by law enforcement to prevent domestic terrorism. Undercover stings usually start with a suspect who has been brought to law enforcement's attention because of hate speech or other suspicious behavior. The suspect may have made comments to an informant, left angry posts on websites, or exchanged e-mails with known extremists. Once a potential suspect has been identified, undercover agents and informants attempt to build a relationship with the suspect.

In 2013, fifty-eight-year-old Terry Lee Loewen, an avionics technician, was arrested after trying to bring a car bomb into a Wichita airport. His arrest came after a months-long undercover sting by FBI agents. Six months prior to his arrest, Loewen began to have conversations with undercover FBI agents. He talked of his desire to commit violent jihad against the United States. Eventually, undercover agents were able to recruit him to use his airport access to plant a bomb. They arrested him before he could execute the plan. Caught in the undercover sting, Loewen was charged with providing support to a terrorist organization and attempting to use a weapon of mass destruction.

The FBI maintains that undercover stings are an important and legal way for agents to prevent potentially deadly acts of domestic terrorism. During a sting, undercover agents and informants have posed as terrorists. They have supplied fake missiles, nonworking suicide vests, fake explosives, and basic training to suspects. Agents pretend to plan a terror plot until they have enough evidence to arrest the suspect.

Entrapment Debate

A debate is growing over whether undercover stings for domestic terrorism have crossed the line to entrapment. Entrapment is a practice whereby a law enforcement agent induces a person to commit an offense the person would have been unlikely to commit otherwise. "If the fragile mental state of an otherwise upstanding individual is exploited to commit a crime that the individual otherwise would not have taken steps to commit, how does that make us safe and why spend taxpayer money on prosecution?" says Dan Monnat, a Kansas defense attorney who questions the FBI's tactics in the Loewen case. "If that is what happened here, we have to ask ourselves is grooming terrorists the best use of our taxpayer money for security if the person otherwise would never have taken further steps in furtherance of terrorism. What is the point?"[63]

In traditional undercover stings, agents may pose as buyers for drug dealers and arms trafficking suspects. The suspects have typically sold drugs or weapons many times before. The sting sets them up to sell the illegal goods once again to an undercover agent. "Prior to 9/11 it would be very unusual for the FBI to present a crime opportunity that wasn't in the scope of the activities that a person was already involved in,"[64] says Mike German of the American Civil Liberties Union, a lawyer and former FBI agent who infiltrated white supremacist groups. In contrast, the suspects in domestic terror cases have usually not committed any previous terroristic acts. In these types of undercover stings, agents are setting suspects up for something new.

In 2010, James Cromitie and three other defendants were found guilty of plotting to detonate explosives near a synagogue and Jewish community center in New York and to launch surface-to-air guided missiles at military planes located at the New York Air National Guard Base in Newburgh, New York. Although Cromitie was a drug dealer who had been known to rant against the Jewish community, he had no violence or hate crimes on his criminal record. To develop a relationship with Cromitie, the FBI used a paid informant who posed as a wealthy Pakistani with ties to a terrorist group. The informant, Shahed Hussain, avoided prison time and deportation in exchange for his undercover work in the investigation. After many months of discussions and the promise of $250,000, Cromitie agreed to plant bombs at two synagogues, along with three associates. Clinton Calhoun III, Cromitie's lawyer, says the informant led his client to violence. "He was searching for answers within his Islamic faith," says Calhoun. "And this informant, I think, twisted that search in a really pretty awful way, sort of misdirected Cromitie in his search and turned him towards violence."[65] The judge in the case agreed that it seemed as if Cromitie had been pushed by the government into participating in the proposed

James Cromitie (center) is escorted out of a federal building by police and FBI officers after being arrested for plotting to bomb synagogues and shoot down military aircraft. His case brought into question the legality of using entrapment techniques to capture terrorists.

attack. "Only the government could have made a 'terrorist' out of Mr. Cromitie, whose buffoonery is positively Shakespearean in its scope,"[66] said Judge Colleen McMahon. Even so, the judge rejected Cromitie's claim of entrapment and sentenced him to twenty-five years in prison.

A DIFFICULT TASK

"For the people in government charged with protecting the homeland against terrorist attacks, the job has never been more difficult. . . . the Boston attack demonstrates how our definition of terrorism has changed—and how the job of defending ourselves has become all the harder."—Andrew Liepman, a senior policy analyst at the RAND Corporation

Andrew Liepman. "Forget What You Think You Know." RAND Corporation, April 19, 2013. www.rand.org/blog/2013/04/forget-what-you-think-you-know.html.

Supporters of sting tactics say preventing domestic terrorism in the United States requires a different approach than traditional drug or weapons investigations. "There isn't a business of terrorism in the United States, thank God," says David Raskin, a former federal prosecutor. "You're not going to be able to go to a street corner and find somebody who's already blown something up." Raskin says agents are not trying "to find somebody who's already engaged in terrorism but find somebody who would jump at the opportunity if a real terrorist showed up in town."[67] Once a suspect cooperates with undercover agents, law enforcement must continue the sting, sometimes for months at a time. "Ignoring such threats is not an option," says Dean Boyd, a Justice Department spokesman, "given the possibility that the suspect could act alone at any time or find someone else willing to help him."[68]

The courts typically have upheld carefully planned sting operations and dismissed defense claims of entrapment in domestic terror cases. For an entrapment claim to be successful, the law requires defendants to show no predisposition to commit the crime, even when encouraged by undercover government agents.

Focused on the Threat

According to a May 2012 Congressional Research Service report, the majority of counterterrorism efforts in the United States have been designed in reaction to acts of foreign terrorism. "9/11 has set the threshold for what terrorism is in the minds of many Americans, and if domestic terrorism lacks the magnitude, it must not be terrorism," says Daryl Johnson, a former counter-terrorism expert at the Department of Homeland Security. Johnson says many in the government are so focused on foreign ji-hadist groups they are not looking at the serious threat posed by domestic terror groups. "What worries me is the fact that our country is under attack from within, from our own radical citizenry," says Johnson. "Yet our leaders don't appear too concerned about this."[69]

Despite the focus on foreign terrorism, domestic terror-ists have been responsible for more crimes in the United States since 9/11. According to the National Counterterrorism Center's Worldwide Incidents Tracking System, of the thirty-five terrorist incidents that occurred in the United States between 2004 and September 2011 more than 70 percent were related to domestic terrorists. As a result, the threat of domestic terrorism can no longer be secondary to foreign threats. Heidi Beirich, director of the Intelligence Project at the Southern Poverty Law Center, agrees that the domestic threat should not be overlooked. "Domestic terrorism is as much a threat as foreign terrorism. The government needs to get serious about this,"[70] she says.

Surveillance Efforts

Intelligence officials say that government surveillance efforts used since the 9/11 attacks have helped prevent many poten-tial terrorist events in the United States. The USA PATRIOT Act expanded the government's ability to conduct antiterrorism surveillance in the United States and abroad. Officials testified before the House Intelligence Committee in 2013 about a plot to blow up the New York Stock Exchange that was stopped be-cause of intelligence gained through expanded domestic sur-

Oklahoma City Bombing

On April 19, 1995, Timothy McVeigh parked a rental truck loaded with a powerful fertilizer bomb in front of the Alfred P. Murrah Federal Building in Oklahoma City, Oklahoma. He quickly left the scene. Minutes later, the bomb exploded in the worst domestic terror attack in the United States. The explosion caused significant damage to the building and killed 168 people, including nineteen children who attended a daycare center in the building.

Timothy McVeigh, a twenty-seven-year-old former army soldier, and his partner in the bombing, Terry Nichols, were members of an extremist right-wing survivalist group. Clashes between the U.S. government and survivalist Randy Weaver in 1992 and the 1993 conflict at the Branch Davidian camp near Waco, Texas, had radicalized McVeigh and Nichols in their suspicion of the U.S. government. The men planned the Oklahoma City bombing to take place on the two-year anniversary of the Waco tragedy. They selected the federal building because it housed several federal agencies, including the Bureau of Alcohol, Tobacco and Firearms (ATF, now called the Bureau of Alcohol, Tobacco, Firearms and Explosives), which had launched the raid on the Branch Davidian camp.

By April 21, investigators had identified and arrested McVeigh and Nichols. They were convicted of multiple counts of murder and conspiracy. In June 2001, McVeigh was executed for his crimes, while Nichols was sentenced to life in prison.

veillance programs. "In recent years, these programs, together with other intelligence, have protected the U.S. and our allies from terrorist threats across the globe to include helping prevent the terrorist—the potential terrorist events over 50 times since 9/11,"[71] said National Security Agency Director Keith Alexander to the committee.

At the same time, surveillance conducted in the name of preventing domestic and foreign terrorism can easily cross the line and violate the privacy and constitutional rights of American citizens. In 2013, U.S. District Court Judge Richard Leon ruled the National Security Agency's bulk collection of metadata—phone records of the time and numbers called without any

Activists protest the surveillance of U.S. citizens by the National Security Agency outside the Department of Justice building in January 2014. Critics accuse the government of violating Americans' privacy and constitutional rights in the fight against terrorism.

disclosure of content—violates privacy rights. "I cannot imagine a more 'indiscriminate' and 'arbitrary invasion' than this systematic and high-tech collection and retention of personal data on virtually every citizen for purposes of querying and analyzing it without prior judicial approval," says Leon. "Surely, such a program infringes on 'that degree of privacy' that the Founders enshrined in the Fourth Amendment."[72]

Preventing the Next Attack

Domestic terror threats are complex and diverse. The next violent attack may come from any number of groups, ideologies, and individuals. Because of law enforcement and citizen efforts, many domestic terror plots have been averted before anyone was hurt or any property was damaged. As long as the threat of domestic terror exists, law enforcement officials will continue to work diligently to protect the United States and its citizens from the next attack.

THE FUTURE OF DOMESTIC TERRORISM

Despite an increased focus on the terror threats since 9/11, domestic terrorism is still an issue in the United States. From the 2012 shooting at the Sikh temple in Oak Creek, Wisconsin, to the 2013 Boston Marathon bombing, recent attacks by domestic terror groups and individuals demonstrate domestic terrorism poses a significant threat in the United States. "The threat has changed from simply worrying about foreigners coming here to worrying about people in the United States, American citizens, raised here, born here, and who, for whatever reason, have decided that they are going to become radicalized and take up arms against the nation in which they were born,"[73] says U.S. Attorney General Eric Holder, pointing out that in the two years previous, 50 of the 126 people indicted on terrorism charges were U.S. citizens.

Experts warn that domestic terrorism from all types of extremist groups is a growing concern. The Congressional Research Service reports there was an apparent increase in homegrown jihadist terror activity between 2009 and 2012, with arrests being made for forty-two homegrown jihadist terror plots by American citizens or legal permanent residents of the United States. Two of these plots became successful attacks. "The apparent rise in such activity after April 2009 suggests that at least some Americans—even if a tiny minority—are susceptible to ideologies supporting a violent form of jihad,"[74] writes Jerome Bjelopera, a specialist in organized crime and terrorism and author of a 2013 Congressional Research Service report for Congress on American jihadist terrorism.

Right-Wing Extremism

Since 2000, the United States has experienced an increase in right-wing extremism. The right-wing extremist movement includes a variety of militia groups, Holocaust deniers, tax protesters, anti-abortion extremists, sovereign citizens, neo-Nazis, white supremacists, and other hate groups that target racial, ethnic, or religious minorities. According to the Southern Poverty Law Center, the number of anti-government "Patriot" groups soared from 149 in 2008 to an all-time high of 1,360 in 2012. The number of hate groups remained above 1,000 in 2013.

Experts believe the increase in these groups has been caused by anger and fear over the country's weak economy, an increase of immigrants, and the diminishing white majority in the American population. "The growth has just been astounding over the last four years. . . . We've never really seen anything like this in

Members of a neo-Nazi group protest at a 2014 anti-gay rights rally in Pennsylvania. Right-wing extremism has increased noticeably across the United States in the last decade.

any of the groups that we count," said Mark Potok, a senior fellow at the Southern Poverty Law Center, in 2013. "As gun control talk began in the wake of the slaughter in Newtown . . . [the] whole movement, these groups out there, have gone from sort of a red heat to white heat. So we are at a very scary moment. It is very reminiscent at least to me of the months leading up to the Oklahoma City bombing."[75]

An Increasing Threat

"We are looking at the very real possibility of more domestic terrorism along these lines. We've seen it in Europe as well as here. I think this is accelerating, not decelerating."—Mark Potok, senior fellow at the Southern Poverty Law Center

Quoted in "'Swimming Upstream,' White Supremacist Groups Still Strong." CNN.com, August 7, 2012. www.cnn.com/2012/08/07/us/white-supremacist-groups/index.html.

Experts predict the growth of right-wing extremism will continue into the future. Anger over the re-election of Barack Obama and his proposed initiatives on immigration and gun control have fueled the outrage of many right-wing extremists. One group, the United States Patriots Union, wrote a letter to conservative state legislators and said, "Our Federal Government is just a tool of International Socialism now, operating under UN Agendas not our American agenda. This means that freedom and liberty must be defended by the states under their Constitutional Balance of Power, or we are headed to Civil War wherein the people will have no choice but to take matters into their own hands."[76]

New Attackers

In a few years, the perpetrators of terrorist attacks in the United States may be individuals and groups that previously were unknown to law enforcement. Thomas Hegghammer, a fellow at Stanford University's Center for International Security and Co-operation, testified at a hearing before a House Foreign Affairs

Sheriff Doug Gillespie of Las Vegas, Nevada, conducts a press conference in June 2014. The suspects pictured are accused of killing of two police officers in broad daylight, a growing trend in non-group-affiliated terrorism.

subcommittee in 2013 that known terrorist groups are more likely to be tracked by law enforcement. As a result, groups that are currently not on the law enforcement's watch list are more likely to carry out future attacks in the United States. "The main threat in the next 2–3 years is ad-hoc attacks by unaffiliated agents, which are harder to prevent, but less lethal on average," he said. "Future groups . . . might be less visible to our agencies and led by a new generation prone to overestimating their own capabilities. Their chances of success will depend on our continued vigilance and ability to spot such grouplets early"[77] he warned.

Lone Offenders

Sometimes an individual, driven by his or her beliefs, chooses to commit terrorist acts alone, without a larger group's knowledge

Teaching Tolerance

The Southern Poverty Law Center (SPLC), a nonprofit civil rights organization, conducts a program that aims to stop extremist violence before it begins. The Center's program "Teaching Tolerance" strives to create inclusive, nurturing school environments. The program produces and distributes documentary films, books, lesson plans, and other materials that promote tolerance. The program also publishes the award-winning *Teaching Tolerance* magazine twice annually. It has produced award-winning documentary films about the civil rights movement and the struggle for social justice. The films teach students that they can make a difference in the world. The program's materials are provided to schools free of charge.

or support. In some cases, these individuals attempt to join a radical extremist group but are rejected or choose to leave because of differences with the group's members. Other times, the lone offender believes that the group's planned activities are not extreme or violent enough. According to the FBI, most domestic terrorist attacks are planned and carried out by lone offenders.

Lone offender attacks can be just as deadly as domestic terror acts planned and carried out by an organized group. Today's lone offenders have access to a wide array of deadly weapons including machine guns, bombs, and chemical and biological weapons. A single bomb can bring down an airplane, killing hundreds of innocent victims. A single gunman can kill and wound dozens of people.

Until a lone offender reaches out to others for support or guidance, it is nearly impossible to identify the offender. "We in the FBI maintain comprehensive coverage of known domestic terrorist groups and their general membership. But lone offenders pose a significant concern in that they stand on the periphery,"[78] said FBI Associate Deputy Director Kevin L. Perkins in a 2012 Statement Before the Senate Committee on Homeland Security and Governmental Affairs.

JoAnne Chesimard (also known as Assata Shakur) is classified as a domestic terrorist and is the first woman on the FBI's list of most wanted terrorists. She lives in Cuba under political asylum. The reward for her capture was raised to $2 million in 2013.

In recent years, there has been an increase in domestic terror attacks being committed by lone offenders, a trend that experts predict will continue into the future. As a result, law enforcement will need to adjust their strategies and tactics to better track and prevent lone offender domestic terrorism. In his book,

Lone Wolf Terrorism: Understanding the Growing Threat, Jeffrey D. Simon writes:

> No longer can theories on terrorism and strategies on how to deal with the terrorist threat exclude the role of lone wolves, since they are capable of matching, and sometimes exceeding, the impact that 'regular' terrorist groups can have upon a nation. The lone wolf is forcing us to revise our thinking about terrorism and shift away from an almost exclusive focus on terrorist groups and organizations toward a new appreciation for the importance of the individual terrorist.[79]

Empowering Local Partners

Working with local communities is considered to be a critical piece of successfully combating domestic terrorism. People in the community, schools, and local police are more likely to notice when a person begins to embrace extremist convictions and behaviors. By intervening early, before a person commits a violent act, domestic terrorism can be prevented for years into the future. Recognizing the importance of local communities, the White House announced a new strategy in 2011 to fight domestic terrorism called "Empowering Local Partners to Prevent Violent Extremism in the United States." It discusses the federal government's existing efforts to prevent domestic terrorism and highlights the need for the government to work with communities to balance the need for safety and the protection of individual civil rights.

A cornerstone of the strategy is making local communities the first line of defense to protect Americans against violent extremists, aided by federal support and guidance. The White House's plan noted the success of the country's counter-gang program, which has engaged communities nationwide in developing ways to prevent gang activity in local neighborhoods. It proposes this model should be used for communities trying to prevent citizens

Somali Muslims and other community members enjoy a soccer field built at the behest of the Somali Education and Special Advocacy Center, a youth advocacy program in Minneapolis, Minnesota. Reaching out to young people is one way communities may prevent youth from becoming radicalized.

and residents from following any ideology that leads to the murder of innocent people. President Barack Obama's deputy national security advisor at the time, Denis McDonough, said:

> Our belief that putting communities in the front here is just recognition, frankly, the fact of life . . . that it's going to be communities that recognize abnormal behavior. . . . So we think that by prioritizing the threat, by training, by providing broad training applicable to the threat broadly, and by saying to communities, "Hey we're going to rely on you as we do on identifying truancy being an early warning indicator for gang violence," for an example—truancy is also going to be an early warning sign for violent extremism.[80]

Using Technology

In the future, experts believe that technology will play an increasingly important role in preventing and investigating domestic terrorism. Technology that allows agents to work faster and share critical information with multiple partners across multiple agencies will improve their ability to prevent and investigate domestic terrorism. The FBI is working to improve and update its technology and systems to better support its agents. New technology introduced at the FBI for the Next Generation Identification System allows agents to process fingerprint transactions faster and with greater accuracy. The FBI also has linking multiple data sets throughout the agency so that agents can search multiple databases more efficiently during an investigation, allowing them to find, process, and pass along important information to law enforcement partners.

In 2012, the FBI also rolled out Sentinel, an information and case management system, to all employees. Sentinel allows the FBI to move all records onto a digital platform, enabling agents to more easily link related cases through digital search abilities. Sentinel's electronic workflow also makes important intelligence available to agents and analysts more quickly, which can allow agents to act on a threat before a suspect or group commits an act of domestic terror.

In Minnesota, local police have been using similar tactics to address the threat of violent Islamist extremism. After more than twenty-one men left the Minneapolis area since 2007 to join a terrorist organization based in Somalia, the police have been participating in regular outreach programs with the local Somali community. They have also launched after-school study programs, open gyms, and arts and crafts projects to engage youth in productive activities and minimize the risk of radicalization. "We have long worked to combat threats to our youth that have become all too familiar—alcohol abuse, drug abuse and gang violence," says Tom Smith, chief of the St. Paul, Minnesota police department. "As we have committed to combating those threats, the St. Paul police department committed to battling a new one—the potential radicalization of our Somali-American youth."[81]

In December 2011 the White House released a Strategic Implementation Plan for the initiative. The plan had three major objectives: enhancing federal community engagement efforts; developing greater government and law enforcement expertise for preventing violent extremism; and countering violent extremist propaganda. Although the plan announced specific actions to accomplish its objectives and designated department leads, critics point out that more guidance is still needed. In a joint statement, Senator Joe Lieberman of Connecticut and Senator Susan Collins of Maine said:

> We appreciate the Administration's latest effort, but much more needs to be done and at a far faster pace given the threat: we still need to know who is directing the 'leads,' what specifically the 'leads' will do, what the time frame is for accomplishing these actions, what resources are necessary, and how to measure success. In addition, we remain troubled that the Administration has not designated one agency to coordinate operations and ensure accountability and effectiveness of the national effort to counter violent Islamist extremism at home.[82]

The Faith Community Working Group

In Montgomery County, Maryland, in 2013, a local initiative kicked off to counter radicalization in the community. The Faith Community Working Group (FCWG) is a community-led initiative dedicated to public safety and preventing violent extremism. FCWG members include local police, government officials, counselors, youth activists, faith leaders, and violence-prevention experts.

When an individual is identified as potentially becoming radicalized, regardless of the reason, he or she is referred to a community partner who is best able to counsel him or her away from violence. If the partner is unsuccessful in counseling the individual, the partner must refer the person back to law enforcement to ensure the community's safety.

Many people believe the program holds great promise. Several local imams (Muslim religious leaders) have shown their commitment to participating in an intervention. Counselors are equipped to advise individuals suffering from social alienation or psychological disorders. Says Hedieh Mirahmadi, president of the World Organization for Resource Development and Education:

> Whether it's in the tragic reality of the Boston terror attack or the Newtown school shooting, we are reminded of the need to build awareness about the social, psychological, and ideological factors that can lead to violent extremism and about the need to enlist community experts to help deal with these factors. Likewise, particularly in the case of the marathon bombing, we see how faith communities must create the space within their institutions to address these issues.[83]

FUTURE ATTACKS

"We live in an age of terrorism that requires individual and collective sacrifices. However, economic and other considerations have distracted the national debate about homeland security away from acknowledgement of a simple, self-evident truth about the evolving threat: the inevitability of successful future attacks by US persons on US soil, targeting US civilians."—J. Michael Barrett, a principal with the Washington, DC-based consulting firm Diligent Innovations and former director of strategy for the White House Homeland Security Council

J. Michael Barrett. "Frontlines: Telling Trends in Domestic Terrorist Threats." *HS Today*, February 1, 2011. www.hstoday.us/focused-topics/counternarcotics-terrorism-intelligence/single-article-page/frontlines-telling-trends-in-domestic-terrorist-threats/5f6ae828eb630efc708feed91cc72be4.html.

Is It Enough?

Although law enforcement has been successful in stopping many domestic terrorists before they act violently, many people fear a large-scale domestic terror act will impact the United States in the future. Experts say the current U.S. strategy for domestic terrorism is not enough and the country needs to do more to protect itself from domestic threats. There is no single point of coordination for the various counterterrorism initiatives at the local, state, and federal levels.

A militia member wears a uniform with the group's insignia at a militia camp outside Detroit, Michigan. Some militias are seen as potential sources of domestic terrorism that are difficult for law enforcement to track. But the growth of militias around the United States can be attributed to citizens' desire to protect themselves in the event of a terrorist attack.

In addition, little has been done to address the causes of domestic terrorism. Rather than trying to prevent an attack after a person has become an extremist, a more effective prevention strategy could address the factors that lead an individual to become a violent extremist. Factors such as social alienation, psychological disorders, political grievances, and foreign terror group ideologies could be addressed and mitigated before a plan of violence even begins.

In addition, current U.S. laws and policies are designed for preventing foreign terrorism and are significantly more powerful than those used to investigate U.S. citizens in connection with domestic terror plots. Weaker laws may limit ways investigators can work on domestic terror cases. According to J. Michael Barrett, a principal with the Washington, D.C.-based consulting firm Diligent Innovations and former director of strategy for the White House Homeland Security Council:

> This reality negatively impacts all manner of analytical activities, including requesting and receiving wiretaps on U.S. persons of interest, as well as policies preventing many law enforcement agencies from keeping names and other identifiable information about U.S. persons on file without associating them to a specific investigation. Indeed, we generally don't even keep identifiable information on people turned away from security checkpoints or found trespassing near critical infrastructure unless there is a clear nexus to a specific threat or other laws are broken. As a result, our ability to "connect" those elusive pre-attack "dots" remains severely constrained.[84]

Understanding the sources of domestic terrorism, their methods, and goals can help law enforcement prevent the next attack on American soil. "While it is unrealistic to expect that we can ever totally defeat terrorism, it is not unrealistic to believe that we can be better prepared to deal with all types of terrorist contingencies,"[85] says Jeffrey Simon.

Introduction

1. Quoted in "102 Hours in Pursuit of Marathon Suspects." *Boston Globe*, April 28, 2013. www.bostonglobe.com/metro /2013/04/28/bombreconstruct/VbSZhzHm35yR88EVm VdbDM/story.html.
2. Quoted in J.M. Hirsch. "Boston Bombing Overview: The Unfolding of A 5-Day Manhunt for Suspects." *Huffington Post*, April 21, 2013. www.huffingtonpost.com/2013/04/21 /boston-bombing-timeline_n_3127079.html.
3. Quoted in "102 Hours in Pursuit of Marathon Suspects."
4. Quoted in Michael Cooper, Michael S. Schmidt, and Eric Schmitt. "Boston Suspects Are Seen As Self-Taught and Fueled By Web." *New York Times*, April 23, 2013. www.nytimes.com/2013/04/24/us/boston-mar athon-bombing-developments.html?pagewanted =1&_r=2.
5. Jack Levin. "Domestic Terrorism: Myths and Realities." *Huffington Post*, May 1, 2013. www.huffingtonpost.com /jack-levin-phd/domestic-terrorism_b_3192124.html.
6. Andrew Liepman. "Forget What You Think You Know." RAND Corporation, April 19, 2013. www.rand.org/blog /2013/04/forget-what-you-think-you-know.html.

Chapter 1: What Is Domestic Terrorism?

7. Brian Michael Jenkins. "A Briefing on Terrorism Issues to New Members of the 112th Congress." RAND Corporation, January 8, 2011. www.rand.org/content/dam/rand/pubs /corporate_pubs/2011/RAND_CP625.pdf.
8. Gordon Lederman and Kate Martin. "The Threat from Within: What Is the Scope of Homegrown Terrorism?" *ABA Journal*, July 1, 2012. www.abajournal.com/magazine/arti

cle/the_threat_from_within_what_is_the_scope_of_home grown_terrorism.

9. Quoted in "Nine Members of a Militia Group Charged with Seditious Conspiracy and Related Offenses." FBI.gov, March 29, 2010. www.fbi.gov/detroit/press-releases/2010 /de032910.htm.

10. Quoted in "Curfew in Effect as Seattle Struggles to Control WTO protests." CNN.com, November 30, 1999. www.cnn .com/US/9911/30/wto.04/index.html?iref=newssearch.

11. Quoted in Byron Pitts. "A Look at the Sovereign Citizen Movement." CBS News.com, September 17, 2012. www .cbsnews.com/news/a-look-at-the-sovereign-citizen -movement/4.

12. Quoted in Pitts. "A Look at the Sovereign Citizen Movement."

13. Quoted in Nick Madigan. "Cries of Activism and Terrorism in S.U.V. Torching." *New York Times*, August 31, 2003. www.nytimes.com/2003/08/31/us/cries-of-activism-and -terrorism-in-suv-torching.html.

14. Quoted in "Arkansas Man Sentenced for His Role in the Firebombing of Interracial Couple's Home." FBI.gov, January 27, 2012. www.fbi.gov/littlerock/press-releases/2012 /arkansas-man-sentenced-for-his-role-in-the-firebombing -of-interracial-couples-home.

15. Scott Stewart. "Domestic Terrorism: A Persistent Threat in the United States." Stratfor.com, August 23, 2012. www .stratfor.com/weekly/domestic-terrorism-persistent-threat -united-states.

Chapter 2: Islamic Terrorists in the United States

16. John McHugh. "Letter to The Honorable Joe Wilson." November 1, 2013. http://media.nbcbayarea.com/documents /Rep-Wilson-letter.pdf.

17. Quoted in "Lawmaker: Report Shows FBI Ignored Accused Fort Hood Shooter Nidal Hasan out of Political Correctness." CBS News.com, July 19, 2012. www.cbsnews.com /news/lawmaker-report-shows-fbi-ignored-accused-fort -hood-shooter-nidal-hasan-out-of-political-correctness.

18. Quoted in David Johnston and Scott Shane. "U.S. Knew of Suspect's Tie to Radical Cleric." *New York Times*, November 9, 2009. www.nytimes.com/2009/11/10/us/10inquire .html?_r=0.

19. Ally Pregulman and Emily Burke. "Homegrown Terrorism." Center for Strategic and International Studies, April 2012. http://csis.org/files/publication/120425_Pregulman _AQAMCaseStudy7_web.pdf.

20. Quoted in Mark Thompson. "Attempted Bombing Was Poorly Plotted, Experts Say." *Time*, May 4, 2010. http://con tent.time.com/time/nation/article/0,8599,1986842,00.html.

21. Jerome P. Bjelopera. "American Jihadist Terrorism: Combating a Complex Threat." Congressional Research Service, January 23, 2013. http://fas.org/sgp/crs/terror/R41416.pdf.

22. Quoted in Bjelopera. "American Jihadist Terrorism."

23. Quoted in Bobby Ghosh. "Most Domestic 'Jihadists' Are Educated, Well-Off." *Time*, Dec. 14, 2009. http://content .time.com/time/nation/article/0,8599,1947703,00.html.

24. Quoted in Ghosh. "Most Domestic 'Jihadists' Are Educated, Well-Off."

25. Pregulman and Burke. "Homegrown Terrorism."

26. Quoted in Sheryl Gay Stolberg and Laurie Goodstein. "Domestic Terrorism Hearing Opens With Contrasting Views on Dangers." *New York Times*, March 10, 2011. www .nytimes.com/2011/03/11/us/politics/11king.html?_r=0.

27. Quoted in Dave Gilson. "Charts: How Much Danger Do We Face From Homegrown Jihadist Terrorists?" *Mother Jones*, April 24, 2013. www.motherjones.com/politics/2013/04 /charts-domestic-terrorism-jihadist-boston-tsarnaev.

28. Quoted in "Study: Threat of Muslim-American Terrorism in U.S. Exaggerated." CNN.com, January 6, 2010. www.cnn .com/2010/US/01/06/muslim.radicalization.study.

29. Peter Bergen and Andrew Lebovich. "Study Reveals the Many Faces of Terrorism." New America Foundation, September 10, 2011. http://newamerica.net/node/57514.

30. Quoted in Stolberg and Goodstein. "Domestic Terrorism Hearing Opens."

31. Quoted in "U.S. Muslim Groups Slam Radicalization Hear-

ings." CNN.com, March 9, 2011. www.cnn.com/2011/POL
ITICS/03/09/radicalization.hearings.

32. Quoted in Charlie Spiering. "Obama: Increase in Domestic
    Terrorism Fueled by Internet." *Washington Examiner*, May
    23, 2013. http://washingtonexaminer.com/obama-increase
    -in-domestic-terrorism-fueled-by-internet/article/2530391.

Chapter 3: Eco-Terrorism

33. Quoted in Bill Morlin. "Woman Long Sought in Largest
    'Eco-Terror' Case Arrested." Southern Poverty Law Center,
    November 29, 2012. www.splcenter.org/blog/2012/11/29
    /woman-long-sought-in-largest-eco-terror-case-arrested.

34. Quoted in Sandro Contenta. "The Rise and Fall of 'Eco-
    Terrorist' Rebecca Rubin." *Toronto Star*, February 2, 2014.
    www.thestar.com/news/insight/2014/02/02/the_rise_and
    _fall_of_ecoterrorist_rebecca_rubin.html.

35. Quoted in Helen Jung, "Eco-Saboteur Rebecca Rubin Gets
    5-Year Federal Prison Sentence." *The Oregonian*, January 27,
    2014. www.oregonlive.com/portland/index.ssf/2014/01
    /eco-saboteur_rebecca_rubin_get.html.

36. Quoted in Jung, "Eco-Saboteur Rebecca Rubin."

37. Quoted in "Animal Rights Extremists Target the Univer-
    sity of California." Anti-Defamation League, March 18,
    2009. http://archive.adl.org/main_extremism/university_of
    _california_animal_rights_extremismc089-2.html.

38. Quoted in "An Overview of Bombing and Arson Attacks by
    Environmental and Animal Rights Extremists in the United
    States, 1995–2010." National Consortium for the Study of
    Terrorism and Responses to Terrorism, May 2013. www
    .start.umd.edu. http://www.start.umd.edu/sites/default/files
    /files/publications/START_BombingAndArsonAttacksBy
    EnvironmentalAndAnimalRightsExtremists_May2013.pdf.

39. Quoted in "Exclusive: Facing Seven Years in Jail, Environ-
    mental Activist Daniel McGowan Speaks Out About the
    Earth Liberation Front, the Green Scare and the Govern-
    ment's Treatment of Activists as 'Terrorists.'" *Democracy
    Now*, June 11, 2007. www.democracynow.org/2007/6/11
    /exclusive_facing_seven_years_in_jail.

40. Quoted in "Interview: Rik Scarce, Author of 'Eco-Warriors.'" PBS.org, September 6, 2011. www.pbs.org/pov/protest-or -terrorism/eco-warriors-rik-scarce-interview.php.

41. Quoted in "Interview: Rik Scarce."

42. Quoted in John Anderson. "Activist or Terrorist, Rendered in Red, White, and Green." *New York Times*, June 8, 2011. www.nytimes.com/2011/06/12/movies/if-a-tree-falls-docu mentary-by-marshall-curry.html?_r=0.

43. Quoted in Karen Eng. "Green Is the New Red: Will Pot- ter on the Problem of Treating Environmentalists as Ter- rorists." TED.com, January 31, 2014. http://blog.ted.com /2014/01/31/will-potter-on-of-treating-environmentalists -like-terrorists.

44. Quoted in "'If a Tree Falls' in Context." PBS.org, Septem- ber 13, 2011. www.pbs.org/pov/ifatreefalls/photo_gallery _background.php?photo=2.

45. Quoted in Anderson. "Activist or Terrorist."

Chapter 4: Domestic Terror Online

46. Quoted in Scott Bauer and Todd Richmond. "Wis. Gun- man Wade Michael Page Urged White Supremacists to Act." *Christian Science Monitor*, August 7, 2012. www.csmonitor .com/USA/Latest-News-Wires/2012/0807/Wis.-gunman -Wade-Michael-Page-urged-white-supremacists-to-act-video.

47. Quoted in Spiering, "Obama: Increase in Domestic Terror- ism."

48. Quoted in "Countering Online Radicalization in America." Bipartisan Policy Center, December 2012. http://bipartisan policy.org/sites/default/files/BPC%20_Online%20Radical ization%20Report.pdf.

49. Quoted in "Countering Online Radicalization in America."

50. Quoted in Seth Jones. "Awlaki's Death Hits Al-Qaeda's So- cial Media Strategy." BBC.com, September 30, 2011. www .bbc.com/news/world-us-canada-15133575.

51. Lederman and Martin. "The Threat from Within."

52. Quoted in "Countering Online Radicalization in America."

53. Quoted in Bob Drogin and Tina Susman. "Internet Mak- ing It Easier to Become a Terrorist." *Los Angeles Times*,

March 11, 2010. http://articles.latimes.com/2010/mar/11 /nation/la-na-internet-jihad12-2010mar12.

54. Quoted in Jim Edwards. "UK Prime Minister Wants to Block British People From Seeing 'Extremist' Web Sites." *Business Insider*, November 26, 2013. www.businessinsider.com /uk-ban-on-extremist-web-sites-2013-11#ixzz2yC3y1Aae.

55. Edward J. Eberle, "What Speech Laws Say." *New York Times*, June 11, 2009. http://roomfordebate.blogs.nytimes .com/2009/06/11/hate-crimes-and-extremist-politics.

56. Phyllis Gerstenfeld, "Don't Overreact." *New York Times*, June 11,2009. http://roomfordebate.blogs.nytimes.com/2009/06 /11/hate-crimes-and-extremist-politics.

57. Gary Shapiro, "Keeping Speech Free On the Internet." *Washington Times*, October 20, 2013. www.washington times.com/news/2013/oct/20/shapiro-keeping-speech free-on-the-internet.

58. Quoted in "Countering Online Radicalization in America."

59. Rob Finch and Kory Flowers. "Violent Domestic Extremism and the Role of Social Media Within Law Enforcement." *The Police Chief* 80 (June 2013): 32–34.

Chapter 5: Preventing Domestic Terrorism

60. Quoted in "Protecting America from Terrorist Attack: The Case of the Homegrown Terrorist." FBI.gov, August 2, 2006. www.fbi.gov/news/stories/2006/august/homegrown _080206.

61. "Domestic Terrorism in the Post-9/11 Era." FBI.gov, September 7, 2009. www.fbi.gov/news/stories/2009/september /domterror_090709.

62. Quoted in "President Bush Signs Anti-Terrorism Bill." PBS. org, October 26, 2001. www.pbs.org/newshour/updates /terrorism-july-dec01-bush_terrorismbill.

63. Quoted in Roxana Hegeman. "Undercover Stings Used to Fight Domestic Terrorism." Yahoo.com, December 14, 2013. http://news.yahoo.com/undercover-stings-used-fight -domestic-terrorism-230404894.html.

64. Quoted in David K. Shipler, "Terrorist Plots, Hatched by the F.B.I." *New York Times*, April 28, 2012. www.nytimes

.com/2012/04/29/opinion/sunday/terrorist-plots-helped
-along-by-the-fbi.html?pagewanted=all&_r=2&.

65. Quoted in Shipler. "Terrorist Plots, Hatched by the F.B.I."
66. Quoted in Shipler. "Terrorist Plots, Hatched by the F.B.I."
67. Quoted in Shipler. "Terrorist Plots, Hatched by the F.B.I."
68. Quoted in Shipler. "Terrorist Plots, Hatched by the F.B.I."
69. Quoted in Sumit Galhotra. "Domestic Terror: Are We Doing Enough to Combat the Threat from Within?" CNN
.com, September 17, 2012. www.cnn.com/2012/09/16/us
/domestic-terrorism.
70. Quoted in Galhotra. "Domestic Terror: Are We Doing
Enough."
71. Quoted in Sean Sullivan. "NSA Head: Surveillance Helped
Thwart More than 50 Terror Plots." *Washington Post*, June
18, 2013. www.washingtonpost.com/blogs/post-politics/wp
/2013/06/18/nsa-head-surveillance-helped-thwart-more
-than-50-terror-attempts.
72. Quoted in Bill Mears and Evan Perez. "Judge: NSA Domestic Phone Data-Mining Unconstitutional." CNN.com, December 16, 2013. www.cnn.com/2013/12/16/justice/nsa
-surveillance-court-ruling.

Chapter 6: The Future of Domestic Terrorism

73. Quoted in Michael Sheridan. "Attorney General Eric Holder Warns: The Real Threat to United States Is American-
Born Terrorists." *New York Daily News*, December 21, 2010.
www.nydailynews.com/news/national/attorney-general
-eric-holder-warns-real-threat-united-states-american
-born-terrorists-article-1.473469.
74. Quoted in Bjelopera. "American Jihadist Terrorism."
75. Quoted in Clare Kim. "Domestic Terrorism: 'Patriot' Hate
Groups Skyrocket." MSNBC.com, March 6, 2013. http://
www.msnbc.com/the-last-word/domestic-terrorism
-patriot-hate-groups-sky.
76. Quoted in Mark Potok, "The Year in Hate and Extremism." Southern Poverty Law Center, Spring 2013. www.spl
center.org/home/2013/spring/the-year-in-hate-and
-extremism.

77. Thomas Hegghammer, "The Future of Anti-Western Jihadism," House Foreign Affairs Committee, July 18, 2013. http://docs.house.gov/meetings/FA/FA18/20130718/1011 55/HHRG-113-FA18-Wstate-HegghammerT-20130718 .pdf.

78. Kevin Perkins. "Statement Before the Senate Committee on Homeland Security and Governmental Affairs," FBI.gov, September 19, 2012. www.fbi.gov/news/testimony/home land-threats-and-agency-responses.

79. Jeffrey D. Simon. *Lone Wolf Terrorism: Understanding the Growing Threat.* Amherst, NY: Prometheus Books, 2013. pp. 20–21.

80. Quoted in Eileen Sullivan, "White House 'Violent Extremism' Strategy to Combat Al Qaeda, Other Radical Groups." *Huffington Post*, August 3, 2011. www.huffingtonpost.com /2011/08/03/white-house-violent-extremism-strategy _n_916911.html.

81. Quoted in Sullivan. "White House 'Violent Extremism' Strategy."

82. Quoted in Sullivan. "White House 'Violent Extremism' Strategy."

83. Hedieh Mirahmadi. "An Innovative Approach to Countering Violent Extremism." Washington Institute, October 9, 2013. www.washingtoninstitute.org/policy-analysis/view/an -innovative-approach-to-countering-violent-extrem ism1.

84. J. Michael Barrett. "Frontlines: Telling Trends in Domestic Terrorist Threats." *HSToday*, February 1, 2011. www .hstoday.us/focused-topics/counternarcotics-terrorism -intelligence/single-article-page/frontlines-telling-trends -in-domestic-terrorist-threats/5f6ae828eb630efc708feed9 1cc72be4.html.

85. Simon. *Lone Wolf Terrorism*, p. 22.

Chapter 1: What Is Domestic Terrorism?

1. In what ways does domestic terrorism differ from other criminal activity?
2. According to the author, what is the goal of sovereign citizens?
3. How does the killing of abortion doctors and clinic workers by anti-abortion extremists undermine the argument that abortion is wrong?

Chapter 2: Islamic Terrorists in the United States

1. According to the author, why have homegrown Islamic extremists become more common?
2. According to the author, what factors affect radicalization?
3. Why is the FBI's use of paid informants controversial?

Chapter 3: Eco-Terrorism

1. What does lawyer Lauren Regan mean when she says that using the word "terrorism" in eco-attacks "really diminishes the power and importance of the word"?
2. According to the author, why are eco-terrorists often difficult for law enforcement to identify?
3. According to the author, what are eco-terrorists trying to accomplish with their actions?

Chapter 4: Domestic Terror Online

1. How has the Internet made it easier for extremists to become violent?

2. How can the Internet be used by investigators to prevent domestic terror attacks?

3. Why is shutting down an extremist website considered a violation of the First Amendment?

Chapter 5: Preventing Domestic Terrorism

1. How does the USA PATRIOT Act enable law enforcement to investigate suspected domestic terrorism plots more effectively?

2. According to the author, what is the difference between domestic terrorism sting operations and traditional sting operations? How does this relate to the idea of entrapment?

3. Why are some people opposed to government surveillance in the name of preventing terrorism?

Chapter 6: The Future of Domestic Terrorism

1. According to the author, what factors have driven the growth of right-wing extremism since 2000?

2. Why are lone offenders considered just as dangerous as, and in some cases more dangerous than, terrorist organizations?

3. How does the Faith Community Working Group work to prevent extremism?

Anti-Defamation League

phone: 212-885-7700

website: www.adl.org

The Anti-Defamation League is one of the nation's premier civil rights and human relations agencies. ADL fights all forms of bigotry and hate, defending civil rights for all citizens.

Federal Bureau of Investigation (FBI)

FBI Headquarters
935 Pennsylvania Avenue, NW
Washington, D.C. 20535
phone: (202) 324-3000
website: www.fbi.gov

The FBI is the lead domestic terrorism agency in the United States. It works to identify and prevent domestic terrorism acts before they occur and investigates them when they do take place.

RAND Corporation

1776 Main Street
P.O. Box 2138
Santa Monica, CA 90407
phone: (310) 393-0411
fax: (310) 393-4818
website: www.rand.org

RAND Corporation is a nonprofit organization that conducts research on a variety of topics, including domestic terrorism and homeland security.

Southern Poverty Law Center

400 Washington Avenue
Montgomery, AL 36104

phone: (334) 956-8200

website: www.splcenter.org

The Southern Poverty Law Center monitors hate groups and other extremists throughout the United States and exposes their activities to law enforcement agencies, the media, and the public.

U.S. Department of Homeland Security (DHS)

245 Murray Lane, SW

Washington, D.C. 20528

phone: 202-282-8000

website: www.dhs.gov

Formed after the 9/11 terrorist attacks, the DHS's main goal is to protect the United States and its citizens from the many threats faced each day.

Books

Diane Andrews Henningfeld. *The Oklahoma City Bombing*. Farmington Hills, MI: Greenhaven, 2012.

Jack Levin and John Levin. *Domestic Terrorism*. New York: Chelsea House, 2006.

Jeffrey D. Simon. *Lone Wolf Terrorism: Understanding the Growing Threat*. Amherst, NY: Prometheus Books, 2013.

Articles

Sandro Contenta. "The Rise and Fall of 'Eco-Terrorist' Rebecca Rubin." *The Toronto Star*, February 2, 2014. www.thestar.com/news/insight/2014/02/02/the_rise_and_fall_of_ecoterrorist_rebecca_rubin.html.

Gordon Lederman and Kate Martin. "The Threat from Within: What Is the Scope of Homegrown Terrorism?" *ABA Journal*, July 1, 2012. www.abajournal.com/magazine/article/the_threat_from_within_what_is_the_scope_of_homegrown_terrorism.

David K. Shipler. "Terrorist Plots, Hatched by the F.B.I." *New York Times*, April 28, 2012. www.nytimes.com/2012/04/29/opinion/sunday/terrorist-plots-helped-along-by-the-fbi.html?pagewanted=all&_r=2&.

Internet Sources

Jerome P. Bjelopera. "American Jihadist Terrorism: Combating a Complex Threat." Congressional Research Service, January 23, 2013. http://fas.org/sgp/crs/terror/R41416.pdf.

Jerome P. Bjelopera. "The Domestic Terrorist Threat: Background and Issues for Congress." Congressional Research Service,

Janaury 17, 2013. http://fas.org/sgp/crs/terror/R42536.pdf.

Ally Pregulman and Emily Burke. "Homegrown Terrorism." Center for Strategic and International Studies, April 2012. http://csis.org/files/publication/120425_Pregulman_AQAM CaseStudy7_web.pdf.

Websites

Anti-Defamation League: Combating Hate (www.adl.org /combating-hate). This site offers a variety of articles and information about domestic terrorism, hate crimes, cyberhate, and law enforcement efforts to prevent extremist crimes.

Federal Bureau of Investigation: Domestic Terrorism (www .fbi.gov/news/stories/2009/september/domterror_090709). This section of the FBI website offers articles and information about a variety of domestic terrorism issues, including past cases and prevention efforts.

Oklahoma City National Museum and Memorial (www .oklahomacitynationalmemorial.org). This website includes video interviews, articles, a history of the bombing, photographs, and other information about the Oklahoma City bombing.

Southern Poverty Law Center: Hate and Extremism (www .splcenter.org/what-we-do/hate-and-extremism). This section of the Center's website offers information and news about hate and extremist groups operating in the United States.

INDEX

A

Activism *vs.* terrorism, 51–53
Al Qaeda, 15, 30, 56, 68
Anarchists, 17–18
Animal Liberation Front
   (ALF), 40, 43, 44, *44*, 44–45
Anti-abortion extremists and
   attacks, 11, 19, 24, 82
Awlaki, Anwar al-, 57–58, *58*

B

Barbarash, David, 40
Bledsoe, Carlos (Adbulhakim
   Muhammad), *34*, 35
Boston Marathon bombing,
   6–7, *7*, 9–10, 29, 37, 81

C

Centennial Olympic Park
   (Atlanta, GA) bombing, 19
Chesimard, JoAnne (Assata
   Shakur), *86*
Civilian targets, 9–10, 11–13
Controversial informants, 36
Cromitie, James, 75–77, *76*
Cross, Frazier Glenn, 22

D

Domestic terrorism

defined, 6–7, 11
empowering of local part-
   ners against, 87–90, *88*
entrapment concerns,
   75–77, *76*
focusing on foreign threats,
   78
future attack concerns, 80,
   81, 91–93
new attacker fears, 83–84
prevention, 68–69
tactics, 24–25
*See also specific acts of ter-
   rorism, terrorist groups,
   and ideologies*
Domestic terrorism, online
   free speech concerns,
   63–65, *80*
intelligence agencies and,
   65–67, 89
overview, 54–55
restricting extremist sites,
   62–63
social media and, 57–58,
   60, 66
violent messages, 56–58,
   58
See also Radicalization;
   Surveillance

E
Earth Liberation Front (ELF), 20–21, *21*, 40, 43, *45*, 45–46, 49
Eco-terrorism
  activism *vs.* terrorism, 51–53
  damage by, 46
  effectiveness of tactics, 50–51
  increase in, 42–44
  targets, *47*, 51
  See also specific groups and people

F
The Family (eco-terrorist group), 40–42, *41*
Federal Bureau of Investigation (FBI), 11, 16–17, 66–67, 70–71
Fitzgerald, Patrick J., *69*
Fort Hood (Killeen, TX) massacre, 26–29, *28*, 32, 58
Free speech concerns, 63–65, *80*
Fusion centers, 73, *73*
Future attack concerns, 80, 91–93

H
Hasan, Nidal Malik, 27–29, 32, 33, 58
Holocaust Memorial Museum (Washington, D.C.) shooting, 22

Homeland Security and Governmental Affairs Committee, 15

I
Islamic terrorists in the United States
  alertness over, 29–31, *30*
  controversial informants, 36
  exaggerated threat, 36–38
  Islamic extremists, 9, 14–15
  local partners against, 38–39
  overview, 27–29
  public attention, 42–43
  See also Radicalization

J
Jihadism, 14–15, 31, 81
Joint Terrorism Task Force (JTTF), 68–69, 72–74

K
Kaczynski, Theodore "Unabomber," 14
Ku Klux Klan, 13, 21–22

L
LaRose, Colleen "Jihad Jane," *61*, 61–62

M
Martinez, Antonio, 66–67
McGowan, Daniel, 48–50, *50*
McVeigh, Timothy, 13, 79

Militia extremists, 15–17, 82, *92*

Moose, Justin, 66

N

Neo-Nazis, 10, 82, *82*

Nettles, Gale, 68–69

Nichols, Terry, 13, 79

Non-group-affiliated terrorists, *84*, 84–87, *86*

O

Oklahoma City bombing, 13, 49, 79, 83

R

Radicalization
   against U.S. government, 79
   online radicalization, 58–62, *61*
   overview, 31–33
   prison radicalization, 32
   travel overseas to join terrorist groups. 38–39, *39*
   See also Domestic terrorism, online

Right-wing extremism, 10, 37–38, 62, 82, 82–83

Rogers, Bobby Joe, 24

Rubin, Rebecca, 40–42, *41*

S

September 11, 2001, attacks, 10, 14, 29–30, 37, 52, 78

Shahzad, Faisal, 30–31

Sikh Temple of Wisconsin attack, 54, *55*, 81

Social media, 57–58, 60, 66

Sovereign citizens, 18–20

Surveillance, 66, 73, *73*, 78–80, *80*

T

Teaching Tolerance program (Southern Poverty Law Center), 85

Tsarnaev, Tamerlan and Dzhokhar, 8–9, 29

U

Undercover stings, 36, 49, *66*, 68, 74–75, 77

USA PATRIOT Act (2001), 49, *71*, 71–72, 78

V

Vail, Colorado, arson attack, *41*, 41–42

Vinas, Bryant Neal, 34–35

Von Brunn, James, 62

W

White supremacist groups, 21–24, *23*, 82

World Trade Organization 1999 meeting (Seattle, WA) protests, *17*, 18

PICTURE CREDITS

Cover: © Everett Collection Inc./Alamy
© AFP/Fox News/Getty Images/Newscom, 61
© AP Images, 86
© AP Images/Alan Mothner, 25
© AP Images/Danny Johnston, 34
© AP Images/Don Ryan, 45
© AP Images/Jack Affleck, 41
© AP Images/John Locher, 84
© AP Images/K.M. Chaudary, 39
© AP Images/M. Spencer Green, 69
© AP Images/Morry Gash, 55
© AP Images/Rick Bowmer, 50
© AP Images/Robert Mecea, 76
© AP Images/Steve Ruark, 66
© AP Images/Todd Plitt, 64
© AP Images/Widman, 82
© Bruce R. Bennett/ZUMAPRESS/Newscom, 73
© Chris Bott/Barcroft USA/Getty Images, 92
© Chris Holmes/Time & Life Pictures/Getty Images, 44
© Don Logan/WireImage/Getty Images, 19
© Francis Specker/EPA/Newscom, 21
© Fred Greaves/ZUMAPRESS/Newscom, 48
© Gale, Cengage Learning, 12, 47
© Jahi Chikwendiu/The Washington Post/Getty Images, 88
© Kelvin Ma/Bloomberg via Getty Images, 7
© Luke Frazza/AFP/Getty Images, 71
© Mike Nelson/AFP/Getty Images, 17
© Paul J. Richards/AFP/Getty Images, 28
© Robin Nelson/ZUMA Press/Newscom, 23
© SITE Intelligence Group/AFP/Getty Images/Newscom, 58
© Spencer Platt/Getty Images, 30
© Win McNamee/Getty Images, 80

ABOUT THE AUTHOR

Carla Mooney is the author of several books for young readers. She loves investigating new ideas and learning about the world in which we live. A graduate of the University of Pennsylvania, Mooney lives in Pittsburgh with her husband and her three children.